IN YOUR GARDEN

Books by
V. SACKVILLE-WEST

Poetry

THE LAND
KING'S DAUGHTER
COLLECTED POEMS
SOLITUDE
THE GARDEN

Biography and Criticism

THE EAGLE AND THE DOVE
PEPITA
ANDREW MARVELL
APHRA BEHN
SAINT JOAN OF ARC

Travel

PASSENGER TO TEHERAN
TWELVE DAYS

Miscellaneous

SOME FLOWERS
COUNTRY NOTES
COUNTRY NOTES IN WARTIME
KNOLE AND THE SACKVILLES
NURSERY RHYMES

Fiction

THE EDWARDIANS
ALL PASSION SPENT
GRAND CANYON
THE EASTER PARTY

V. SACKVILLE-WEST

In Your Garden

FRANCES LINCOLN

FRANCES LINCOLN LTD
4 Torriano Mews
Torriano Avenue
London NW5 2RZ
www.franceslincoln.com

First published by
MICHAEL JOSEPH LTD 1951

IN YOUR GARDEN

A CIP catalogue record for this book is available from the British Library.

First Frances Lincoln Edition 2004

ISBN 0 7112 2354 8

Printed in England

2 4 6 8 9 7 5 3 1

Foreword

IT was with some reluctance that I agreed to the publication of these snippets in book-form. They were all very well as they appeared, weekly or at longer intervals according to the space available in the columns of *The Observer*; but when it came to dressing them up into the solidity of a real book with stiff covers and the expectation of a place to itself on somebody's shelves, I quailed at their incompleteness, their repetitiveness, and also at the haphazard way they had been dotted about the years.

Two problems confronted me. Should I amplify them or leave them to stand just as they had appeared? And should I rearrange them, grouping them under months and seasons, although I had not always written them on the seasonal system? In the end I compromised, making a few additions where it seemed desirable and putting the articles into chronological order.

It will readily be understood that neither *The Observer* nor any other journal could have allowed the 'free advertisement' of publishing the names and addresses of nurserymen and seedsmen. This led to considerable exasperation on the part of my readers; 'What is the good of recommending these out-of-the-way things unless you tell us where to obtain them?' It led also to a formidable increase in my correspondence; I think two thousand enquiries arising out of one article was the record, but on several other occasions a thousand letters arrived, done up in bundles of fifty, tied round with string. I trust and

believe that I answered them all. If anyone was overlooked,
I take this opportunity of offering an apology.

Here in this book, where no such restrictions prevail, I
have added most of the appropriate names and addresses,
and have also supplied a short general list in an appendix.
This does not mean that I have attempted to give a comprehensive list of all the nurserymen or seedsmen in our
country. It merely means an indication of where you can
get shrubs, trees, bulbs, roses, flower-seeds, and whatever
you want.

I should like to express my thanks to *The Observer*, both
for printing my articles in the first instance and for allowing
me to reprint them here; to *The Spectator* for permission to
include *A little flower-book*; and to the Editor of the Royal
Horticultural Society's Journal, for permission to include
a note on the garden at Hidcote Manor. I cannot, alas,
extend my thanks to Messrs. Cobden Sanderson, the
original publishers of *Some Flowers* in 1937, since that
most estimable firm went out of business some years ago.

Some of the essays in that book are reprinted here, on
pages 173–217.

V. S.-W.

Sissinghurst Castle,
   Cranbrook, Kent.

Contents

Index of Plants

A

Abelia triflora, 81
Abutilon
  megapotamicum, 199–201
  vitifolium, 201
Acaena, 144
Aethionema Warleyensis, 145
Almond, *see* Amygdalus
Alstroemeria, 85, 88–90
Althea frutex (hibiscus), 81, 88
Amaryllis (Belladonna lily), 131
Ampelopsis Veitchii (Virginia
  creeper), 69
Amygdalus (almond) Pollardii, 109
Anemone
  apenina, 181
  hepatica, 103
  japonica, 104–5
  pulsatilla, 53–4
  St. Bavo, 36
  St. Brigid, 36
Annuals, mixed, 50–1, 54–5, 114,
  133
Aquilegia (columbine), 84, 158
Armeria Corsica (thrift), 145
Artichoke
  Chinese, 98–9, 121
  Globe, 99–100, 121
  Jerusalem, 98
Asperula odorata (sweet wood-
  ruff), 68
Asters (Michaelmas daisy), 133
Aubretia, 70
Auricula, 182–4
Azara microphylla, 51–2

B

Belladonna lily, *see* Amaryllis
Bellis Dresden China, 75, 145
Berberis Thunbergii, 123, 142
Bignonia, 97–8
Buddleia alternifolia, 101
Bullaces, 127

C

Calabrese, 121
Caraway, 121
Caryopteris, 87, 137–8
Ceanothus Gloire de Versailles, 87
Celeriac, 121
Cerasus Lannesiana Ukon, 109
Ceratostigma Willmottiana, 87
Chabaud carnations, 30–1
Chervil, 151
Chimonanthus fragrans (winter-
  sweet), 26
Chionodoxa, 145
Chives, 151
Choisya ternata (Mexican orange-
  blossom), 184
Christmas rose, *see* Helleborus niger
Clematis, 63–4, 105
  flammula, 117
Clerodendron, 101
Clethra alnifolia, 101
Cobaea scandens, 134
Colchicum, 23–5
Columbine, *see* Aquilegia
Cornus florida rubra, 123
  Kousa, 123
Cotoneaster rugosa Henryii, 142
Cotula squalida, 144
Crataegus Crus-Galli, 123

IN YOUR GARDEN

January

SOME generous friend may have given you a plant-token for Christmas, and you may be wondering, as I am now wondering, how best to expend it. A plant-token is a real gift from heaven; it represents an extravagance one might hesitate to commit for oneself; a luxury, an extra, a treat. One has no alternative, for, unlike a cheque, one cannot virtuously put it to the reduction of one's overdraft. There is nothing to be done with it except to buy a plant.

Could one do better than choose the autumn-flowering cherry, *Prunus subhirtella autumnalis?* In England it might more properly be called winter-flowering, for it does not open until November, but in its native Japan it begins a month earlier; hence its autumnal name. Here, if you pick it in the bud and put it in a warm room or a greenhouse, you can have the white sprays in flower six weeks before Christmas, and it will go on intermittently, provided you do not allow the buds to be caught by too severe a frost, until March.

It is perhaps too ordinary to appeal to the real connoisseur—a form of snobbishness I always find hard to understand in gardeners—but its wands of white are of so delicate and graceful a growth, whether on the tree or in a vase, that it surely should not be condemned on that account. It is of the easiest cultivation, content with any reasonable soil, and it may be grown either as a standard or a bush; I think the bush is preferable, because then you get the flowers at eye-level instead of several feet above your head—though it can also look very frail and youthful, high up against the pale blue of a winter sky.

*　*　*

How precious are the flowers of mid-winter! Not the hot-house things, nor even the forced trusses of lilac, most of which, I understand, come from Holland, but the genuine toughs that for some strange reason elect to display them-selves out-of-doors at this time of year. The Winter-sweet opens its yellow star-fish against a wall, and the twisted ribbons of the Witch-hazel are disentangling themselves on their leafless branches. Both of these sweet-scented winter flowerers should qualify for a choice with the plant-token.

Garrya elliptica is not so often seen, though it has been known in this country since 1818; its nickname, the Tassel Bush, describes it best, for it hangs itself from December onwards with soft grey-green catkins eight or ten inches in length, like bunches of enormous caterpillars among the very dark leaves. Some people think it dismal, but a large bush is an imposing sight if you have the patience to wait for it. It does require patience, for it dislikes being moved and, therefore, must be planted small; also you must insist upon getting a male plant, or there will not be any catkins. The female plant will give you only bunches of black fruits. As it will thrive against a north wall, however, where few other things will thrive, it may well be left there to take its time without occupying the space wanted for something else.

January 15, 1950

Someone has been pleading with me to put in a good word for sweet-briar. I do so most willingly, for a hedge of sweet-briar is one of the most desirable things in any garden.

It is thorny enough to keep out intruders, should it be
needed as a boundary protection; in early summer it is as
pretty as the dog-rose, with its pale pink single flowers; in
autumn it turns itself into a sheer wall of scarlet hips; and
on moist muggy evenings after rain the scent is really and
truly strong in the ambient air. You do not need to crush
a leaf between your fingers to provoke the scent: it swells
out towards you of its own accord, as you walk past, like a
great sail filling suddenly with a breeze off those Spice
Islands which Columbus hoped to find.

These are many virtues to claim, but even so we may
add to them. It is the Eglantine of the poets, if you like that
touch of romance. True, Milton seems to have confused it
with something else, probably the honeysuckle:

> . . . through the sweet-briar or the Vine,
> Or the twisted Eglantine. . . .

but what does that matter? it is pedantic to be so precise,
and we should do better to take a hint from Milton and plant
a *mixed* hedge of honeysuckle and sweet-briar, with perhaps an ornamental vine twining amongst them—the
purple-leafed vine, *Vitis vinifera purpurea*, would look
sumptuous among the red hips in October.

I have never seen a hedge of this composition; but why
not? Ideas come to one; and it remains only to put them
into practice. The nearest that I have got is to grow the
common *Clematis Jackmanii* into my sweet-briar, planting
the clematis on the north side of the hedge, where the roots
are cool and shaded and the great purple flowers come
wriggling through southwards into the sun. It looks fine,
and the briar gives the clematis just the twiggy kind of
support it needs.

Sweet-briar is a strong grower, but is often blamed for
going thin and scraggy towards the roots. I find that you
can correct this weakness by planting your hedge in the

first instance against a system of post-and-wire, and subsequently tying-in the long shoots to the posts and wire instead of pruning them. Tie the shoots horizontally, or bend them downwards if need be, thus obtaining a thick, dense growth, which well compensates you for the initial trouble of setting up the posts and the wire. They will last for years, and so will the briar.

The common sweet-briar will cost you 2s. 6d. to 3s. a plant, and the single plant will spread, horizontally, twenty feet or more. The Penzance hybrid briars are more expensive, 4s. 6d. to 5s. each. *Amy Robsart*, with deep rose flowers, and *Lady Penzance*, with coppery-yellow flowers, are particularly to be recommended.

January 22, 1950

It is amusing to make one-colour gardens. They need not necessarily be large, and they need not necessarily be enclosed, though the enclosure of a dark hedge is, of course, ideal. Failing this, any secluded corner will do, or even a strip of border running under a wall, perhaps the wall of the house. The site chosen must depend upon the general lay-out, the size of the garden, and the opportunities offered. And if you think that one colour would be monotonous, you can have a two- or even a three-colour, provided the colours are happily married, which is sometimes easier of achievement in the vegetable than in the human world. You can have, for instance, the blues and the purples, or the yellows and the bronzes, with their attendant mauves and orange, respectively. Personal taste alone will dictate what you choose.

For my own part, I am trying to make a grey, green, and white garden. This is an experiment which I ardently hope may be successful, though I doubt it. One's best ideas seldom play up in practice to one's expectations, especially in gardening, where everything looks so well on paper and in the catalogues, but fails so lamentably in fulfilment after you have tucked your plants into the soil. Still, one hopes.

My grey, green, and white garden will have the advantage of a high yew hedge behind it, a wall along one side, a strip of box edging along another side, and a path of old brick along the fourth side. It is, in fact, nothing more than a fairly large bed, which has now been divided into halves by a short path of grey flagstones terminating in a rough wooden seat. When you sit on this seat, you will be turning your backs to the yew hedge, and from there I hope you will survey a low sea of grey clumps of foliage, pierced here and there with tall white flowers. I visualize the white trumpets of dozens of Regale lilies, grown three years ago from seed, coming up through the grey of southernwood and artemisia and cotton-lavender, with grey-and-white edging plants such as *Dianthus Mrs. Sinkins* and the silvery mats of *Stachys Lanata,* more familiar and so much nicer under its English names of Rabbits' Ears or Saviour's Flannel. There will be white pansies, and white peonies, and white irises with their grey leaves . . . at least, I hope there will be all these things. I don't want to boast in advance about my grey, green, and white garden. It may be a terrible failure. I wanted only to suggest that such experiments are worth trying, and that you can adapt them to your own taste and your own opportunities.

All the same, I cannot help hoping that the great ghostly barn-owl will sweep silently across a pale garden, next summer, in the twilight—the pale garden that I am now planting, under the first flakes of snow.

January 14, 1951

January seems the wrong time of year to think of planting bulbs, but there are some which should be planted in March or April, so this is the moment to order them. I would recommend the Kaffir Lily, officially called *Schizostylis coccinea*, with its pretty pink variety called *Mrs. Hegarty*. It resembles a miniature gladiolus, and it has the advantage, from our point of view, of flowering in October and November, when it is difficult to find anything out of doors for indoor picking.

The Kaffir Lily will cost you anything from seven shillings to eight or nine shillings a dozen. One dozen will give you a good return, if you plant them in the right sort of place and look after them properly. Planting them in the right sort of place means giving them a light, well-drained soil in full sun. Looking after them properly means that you must give them plenty of water during their growing period, when their leaves are throwing up, rather as you would treat an amaryllis, the Belladonna lily. You should realize that they are not entirely hardy, especially in our colder counties; but they are reasonably hardy in most parts of England; a thin quilt of bracken or dry leaves next winter will keep them safe for years. It is remarkable what a little covering of bracken will do for bulbs. Speaking for myself, I cannot imagine anything less adequate than a draughty scatter of bracken on a frosty night, give me a thick eider-down and blankets every time, and a hot-water bottle, too, but bulbs which are buried deep down in the earth will keep themselves warm and safe with the thinnest cover from frost above them.

Another bulb, or corm, you should order now and plant in March is *Tigridia*, the Mexican Tiger-flower. This is a wildly beautiful exotic-looking thing. It throws only one flower at a time, and that flower lasts only one day, but it is of such superlative beauty and is succeeded by so many other blooms, day after day, that it is well worth the 3s. 9d. you will have to pay for a dozen of mixed varieties. A sunny place is essential, and, like dahlias, they should be lifted and stored through the winter.

January 21, 1951

This is the time to think of ordering bulbs of the autumn-flowering crocus. If the nurseryman knows his job, they will not be sent to you until midsummer or even August, but it is advisable to order now in case the supply runs out, or, to put it in more familiar language, get in at the top of the queue.

We are so well accustomed to associating crocuses with Spring that it may come as a surprise to some people to learn that some sorts of crocus will flower with as vernal an appearance from September onwards into November. *Crocus speciosus* is one that should be ordered now; it is cheap to buy, 2s. 6d. a dozen, 17s. 6d. a hundred; I bought a dozen last year and how lovely they were, chalices the colour of Parma violets rejoicing my autumnal heart, coming out in September so unexpectedly to turn autumn into spring. *C. speciosus Cassiopea* comes out later, October–November; *C. speciosus globosus* in November, the latest of all. These are both a little more expensive than the type, at 3s. 6d. a dozen; but do plant even a little patch of six or twelve, in a special corner.

Then there is *Crocus sativus*, the Saffron crocus, a pinkish-lilac colour. How difficult these colour descriptions are! This flowers in October, and costs from 2s. 6d. to 3s. a dozen. If you want something more unusual, there is *C. asturicus atropurpureus*, dark violet, which in a mild winter might go on flowering into December, 4s. a dozen. I am sorry these small things should have to suffer such gigantic names; but when you work it out, you find that *Crocus asturicus atropurpureus* merely means the very dark purple crocus, native to the Asturias province of northern Spain.

I have by no means exhausted the list, and have not even touched on the *Colchicum*, which many people are apt to confuse with the autumn-flowering crocus. The only point in common, for those who do not want to be bothered

with botanical differences, * is that they should both be
ordered now for August delivery. Owing to what we have
been taught to call shortages of newsprint, I shall have to
leave the *Colchicum* till next Sunday, when I can devote
my four hundred words to this most lovely and surprising
race. Messrs. Wallace, Messrs. Barr, and Mr. Ralph Cusack
all have good lists of the crocus and the *Colchicum*. Their
addresses will be found at the end of this book.

* * *

I have no means of thanking the anonymous sender of a
registered packet addressed to me; but if he should happen
to be a reader of these articles, will he please accept my
unspeakable thanks? He (or she?) will understand.

January 28, 1951

The colchicums, as I said, should be ordered now for
summer delivery. They are more expensive than the
crocuses, ranging from 6s. 6d. to 10s. 6d. a dozen, but being
larger they make more effect. A drift of them, especially in
grass, is a brilliant sight in September and October; they
should not be planted on a lawn, as the big leaves which
appear in spring or early summer are unsightly; and do
not plant them where sheep or cattle graze, as they are
poisonous to animals. The ideal place is an orchard, where
their pink or lilac cups will coincide with the apples hanging
overhead, but if the grass is rough remember to cut it just
before the flowers break through or they will be lost to
sight. The end of August is a safe time for this operation.

They do not object to a little light shade, such as would

---

* If you do want to be bothered with botanical differences, the crocus
belongs to the genus *Iridaceae* (irises) and the *Colchicum* to the genus
liliaceae (lilies). Confusion is increased by the fact that *Colchicum autumnale*
is popularly known as the Meadow Saffron, and *Crocus sativus* as the
Saffron Crocus.

be thrown by the fruit trees, but they are equally happy in full sun. It may surprise you that a bulb planted in July or August should leap into flower so soon afterwards, and it may surprise you even more to find that when the bulbs arrive in their paper bag they should already be showing a bleached-looking growth, rather like celery. Do not worry. Cut a hole in the turf, drop the bulbs in, two to three inches deep, stamp the turf down again, and leave them to do what nature intended.

Speciosum and *autumnale* are both good varieties, rosy in colour; there are white forms of these also. *Bornmulleri* and *byzantinus* are magnificent; and one of the finest is the hybrid *Lilac Wonder*, rather more expensive at 10s. 6d. a dozen. Other very fine hybrids are *Rosy Dawn*, bright pink; and *The Giant*, a softer pink; and you can also obtain a mixture of the new hybrids at 10s. 6d. a dozen. I do not care so much for the double-flowered kind, *autumnale roseum plenum*, since I think the beauty of a colchicum or of a crocus, apart from the colour, lies in the pure lines of the goblet-like shape; this, like many other things, is a matter of taste.

A word of practical advice: put a ring of slug bait round each clump as soon as the pale noses appear, and be quick about it, because the pale nose of to-day is the full flower of to-morrow. Otherwise you will wonder how anyone could ever recommend a thing of such rags and tatters.

Messrs. Wallace, and Messrs. Barr and R. Cusack all have good lists of colchicum.

February

February 2, 1947

IN response to many requests, I pursue the subject of plants that will flower out of doors during the winter months. *Chimonanthus fragrans*, in English the Winter-sweet, should have a place of honour. Although it was introduced from China so long ago as 1766, it is not often seen now except in the older gardens, and in honesty I should warn purchasers of young plants that it will not begin to flower until it is five or six years old. But it is worth waiting for. Extremely sweet-scented, even in the cold open air, long sprigs loaded with the strange maroon-and-yellow flowers can be cut all through January and February; it lasts for two or three weeks in water, especially if you smash the stems with a hammer, a hint which applies to all hard-wooded growth. The Winter-sweet will eventually reach to a height of ten feet or more; it is happiest grown against a wall for protection, but I have seen it growing into a big bush in the open in a garden in Kent—not my garden, alas!

The text-books instruct us to prune it hard back to the old wood immediately after it has finished flowering; I obediently followed these instructions for years, and got nothing but some truncated little miseries in consequence; then I rebelled, as all good gardeners should rebel when they find their own experience going against the text-book, and left my Winter-sweet unpruned one year, with the rich reward of longer sprays to cut for indoors. I fancy that

this extravagant cutting will provide all the pruning that
is necessary.

If you are the sort of gardener that likes raising your own
nursery stock, leave a couple of sprays to develop their
gourd-shaped fruit, and sow the seed when ripe in a pot or
pan. It germinates very obligingly.

* * *

I hesitate to insult readers of *The Observer* by recommending the merits of so well known a plant as the winter-
flowering jasmine, *Jasminum nudiflorum*, introduced from
China in 1844. We all grow it now. I picked long sprays of
it on December 4th and all the buds opened indoors in
water, lasting for several weeks. The flowers and buds are
not very frost-resistant out of doors; so here is a hint: grow
a plant of it in a large pot; leave the pot standing out of
doors all summer and autumn; bring the pot indoors in
November; train the shoots round some bamboo canes;
stand the pot on the floor in a corner of your room; don't
forget to water it; put a large plate or bowl under the pot
or your carpet will suffer; and having done all this you may
confidently expect a golden fountain for two or three
months unaffected by the weather outside.

* * *

In a mild season the Algerian Iris, generally called *iris
stylosa*, but, more correctly, *iris unguicularis*, should start
flowering in November and continue until March. They
vary in colour from a lavender blue to a deep purple (there
is also a white form) and are from six to eight inches high.

The clumps should be planted at the foot of a south wall,
full sun, in the most gritty soil imaginable; they love old
mortar rubble, gravel, ashes, broken bricks; they flourish

on a starvation diet; hate being transplanted or otherwise
disturbed; are loved by slugs and snails, so be sure to put
down some meta-and-bran, and pick them while still as
closely furled as an unbroken flag round its flag-staff. They
will then unfurl in the warmth of your room; you can
watch them doing it. *

February 1948

It is agreeable sometimes to turn for a change from the
dutifully practical aspects of gardening to the consideration
of something strange, whether we can hope to grow it for
ourselves or not. A wet January evening seemed just the
time for such an indulgence of dreams, and in an instant
I found my room (which hitherto had boasted only a few
modest bulbs in bowls) filling up with flowers of the queerest
colours, shapes, and habits. The first batch to appear, thus
miraculously conjured out of the air, were all of that
peculiar blue-green which one observes in verdigris on an
old copper, in a peacock's feather, on the back of a beetle,
or in the sea where the shallows meet the deep.

First came a slender South African, *Ixia viridiflora*, with
green flowers shot with cobalt blue and a purple splotch:
this I had once grown in a very gritty pan in a cold greenhouse, and was pleased to see again. Then came the tiny
sea-green Persian iris, only three inches high, which I had
seen piercing its native desert but had never persuaded
into producing a single flower here. Then came *Delphinium
macrocentrum*, an East African, which I had never seen at
all, but which is said to rival the Chilean *Puya alpestris* in
colouring.

Puya alpestris I knew. A ferocious-looking plant, and
reluctant. Seven years had I cherished that thing in a pot,
before it finally decided to flower. Then it threw up a spike
and astonished everybody with its wicked-looking peacock

* See pp. 33–4.

trumpets and orange anthers, and side-shoots on which, apparently, humming-birds were supposed to perch and pollinate the flower.

And now here it was again, in my room, this time accompanied by the humming-birds which had been lamentably absent when I had flowered it after seven years. There were quite a lot of birds in my room by now, as well as flowers. For *Strelitzia reginae* had also arrived, escorted by the little African sun-birds which perch and powder their breast-feathers with its pollen. It is rare for plants to choose birds as pollinators instead of insects; and here were two of them. *Strelitzia reginae* itself looked like a bird, a wild, crested, pointed bird, floating on an orange boat under spiky sails of blue and orange. Although it had been called regina after Queen Charlotte the consort of George III, I preferred it under its other name, the Bird of Paradise Flower.

Then, as a change to homeliness, came clumps of the old primroses I had tried so hard to grow in careful mixtures of leaf-mould and loam, but here they were, flourishing happily between the cracks of the floorboards. Jack-in-the-Green, Prince Silverwings, Galligaskins, Tortoiseshell, Cloth of Gold; and as I saw them there in a wealth I had never been able to achieve, I remembered that the whole primula family was gregarious in its tastes and hated the loneliness of being one solitary, expensive little plant. They like huddling together, unlike the Lichens, which demand so little company that they will grow (in South America at any rate) strung out along the high isolation of telegraph wires.

There seemed indeed no end to the peculiarities of plants, whether they provided special perches for the convenience of their visitors, or turned carnivorous like the Pitcher-plants. Why was it that the Vine grew from left to right in the Northern hemisphere, but refused to grow otherwise than from right to left in the Southern? Why was the poppy called *Macounii* found only on one tiny Arctic island in the Behring Sea and nowhere else in the world? How had it come there in the first place? In a room now overcrowded with blooms of the imagination such speculations flowed easily, to the exclusion of similar speculations on the equally curious behaviour of men.

The walls of the room melted away, giving place to a garden such as the Emperors of China once enjoyed, vast in extent, varied in landscape, a garden in which everything throve and the treasures of the earth were collected in beauty and brotherhood. But a log fell in the fire: a voice said: 'This is the B.B.C. Home Service; here is the news,' and I awoke.

February 5, 1950

The hardy border carnation has long been popular, and with the introduction of the Chabaud carnation its popularity has increased. M. Chabaud was a botanist from Toulon who, in about 1870, raised this hybrid between the old perennial carnation and the annual kind. The seeds of the original Chabaud carnation are now on sale in this country, and certainly ought to be grown by every gardener who has half-a-dozen seed boxes to spare.

There are two sorts, the annual and the perennial. The annuals are divided into the *Giant Chabaud*, the *Enfant de Nice*, and the *Compact Dwarf*. They should be sown in February or March in boxes of well-mixed leaf-mould, soil and sharp sand. They require no heat; but in frosty weather the seedlings should be protected. Do not over-water. Keep them on the dry side. Plant them out when they are large enough, in a sunny place with good drainage. (I think myself that they look best in a bed by themselves, not mixed in with other plants). Their colour range is wide: yellow, white, red, purple, pink, and striped. They are extremely prolific, and if sown in February should be in flower from July onwards. If you care to take the trouble, they can be lifted in October and potted, to continue flowering under glass or indoors on a window-sill, i.e. safely away from frost, well into the winter.

The perennial sort, which is perfectly hardy, should be sown March–June and planted out this summer to flower during many summers to come. Those gardeners who appreciate a touch of historical tradition will be gratified to know that in the variety called *Flamand* they are getting a seventeenth-century strain and may expect the flaked and mottled flower so often seen in those enchanting muddles crammed into an urn in Dutch flower-paintings. Indeed, the catalogue of these seeds is full of romance, not only historical but geographical, if you agree with me that there is something romantic in the thought of Provence, from which your seeds will come. Have you been to St. Remy, that Roman settlement in what was once south-eastern Gaul, where a Roman triumphal arch still stands, and where flowers are now grown in mile-wide stretches for the seed market? It must be a wonderful sight, when all the carnations and zinnias and petunias are in flower, staining the bistred landscape of Van Gogh's Provence in acres of colour.

This is perhaps neither here nor there in an article on practical gardening, but I always get led away in excitement over the plants I recommend. I was led away also by a note in the same catalogue about petunias, a special strain grown by the nuns in a convent near Toulon. I have not tried these yet, but I mean to. I like thinking about those Sisters in Toulon, pottering about their convent garden, saving their petunia seeds, and sending them to us in England for our delight.*

* Alas, in all honesty I must add that the petunias were a disappointment. They were supplied under separate-named colours, but I fear the good nuns must have been too much preoccupied with their devotions to take sufficient care of their seed-crop.

The agent from whom the carnation and petunia may be obtained is George Roberts, Davington Priory, Faversham, Kent.

February 12, 1950

Not everybody, these days, can be bothered with sowing annuals, not even the hardy penny-packet kinds such as clarkia and godetia, which will grow anywhere and make so bright a show throughout the summer. Most people are going in for the permanent things, such as the flowering shrubs, giving less trouble for more reward. I have myself eliminated nearly all annuals from my garden; but there are two which I obstinately retain: the zinnia and the Morning Glory.

These are both half-hardy, which means that you must not risk a spring frost catching them. If you have glass, you can sow them in seed boxes in March or April, but if no glass, then they can be sown out of doors towards the end of May, on the place where they are to flower. Honestly, I don't think you lose much time by adopting this method, and you certainly save yourself a mort of trouble.

I have long since abandoned the practice of sowing zinnias in seed boxes, and I do believe that you get sturdier plants in the long run, when the seedlings have suffered no disturbance. Sow the seeds in little parties of three or four, and thin them remorselessly out when they are about two inches high, till only one lonely seedling remains. It will do all the better for being lonely, twelve inches away from its nearest neighbour. It will branch and bulge sideways if you give it plenty of room to develop, and by August or September will have developed a spread more desirable in plants than in human beings.

Some people do not like zinnias: they think them stiff and artificial-looking. But they are surely no more artificial-looking than dahlias, which they somewhat resemble, and their colours are even more subtle than the colours of the dahlia. In zinnias, you get a mixture of colours seldom seen in any other flower: straw-colour, greenish-white, a particular saffron-yellow, a dusky rose-pink, a coral-pink. The only nasty colour produced by the zinnia is a magenta, and this, alas, is produced only too often. When magenta threatens, I pull it up and throw it on the compost heap, and allow the better colours to have their way.*

The Morning Glory is a joy every year. Those enormous sky-blue trumpets that open every morning before breakfast and shut themselves up again between luncheon and tea. . . . You must make sure to get the right kind: it is called *Ipomea rubra-coerulea*, *Heavenly Blue*. Messrs. Sutton have it.

* * *

Here I should like to add a note which did not appear in *The Observer*, because it is really no use telling the readers of a short article in a weekly journal about things they cannot obtain. It leads only to frustration, indignant letters, and irritability all round.

The seed of a very special form of *Ipomea* was given to me by my friend, Mr. Noel Sutton. What a gift! He had got it from India, and it was called *Ipomea Bona-Nox*. It flowered only at night; so you had to sit up with it if you wanted to catch it in flower. It might have been carved out of the thinnest flakes of ivory.

February 19, 1950

A correspondent writes to suggest that I should supply 'a few extra tips' on growing the Algerian iris. It seems a good idea. They are most obliging plants, even if maltreated, but a little extra kindliness and understanding

* See also pp. 207–9.

will bring forth an even better response. As is true of most
of us, whether plants or humans.

Kindliness, so far as the Algerian iris is concerned,
consists in starving it. Rich cultivation makes it run to leaf
rather than to flower. What it really enjoys is being grown
in a miserably poor soil, mostly composed of old lime and
mortar rubble and even gravel: a gritty mixture at the
foot of a sunny wall, the grittier and the sunnier the better.
Sun and poverty are the two things it likes. To give it the
maximum of sun to ripen itself off during the summer, you
should chop down its leaves in May or early June and let the
sun get at it for so long as our climate allows. There is no
more that you can do for it except to guard it against snails
and slugs. It is vital to do this if the flower is not to be
nibbled and tattered by these creatures, which hibernate so
happily within the leaves and in the cracks of the wall.
Any proprietary slug-bait will do the job for you, or you
can make your own mixture which is far cheaper and just
as efficacious, with Meta tablets, smashed into a fine powder
and mixed with bran, tea-leaves, or even sawdust. It may
be unkind to the snails, but one has to make one's choice.

The Algerian iris is known to most of us as *Iris stylosa*.
It should, in fact, be called *Iris unguicularis*, because this is
the older botanical name for it, *unguiculus* meaning a small
or narrow claw. Do we have to bother about that? Let us,
rather, record that it is the native of stony ground in
Algeria, Greece, Crete, Syria, and Asia Minor, and that it
accommodates itself very willingly to our island, flowering
before Christmas sometimes, especially after a hot, dry
summer, and continuing to flower in mild weather right
into March.* You should search your clumps of the grass-like
leaves every day for possible buds, and pull the promising
bud while it still looks like a tiny, tightly-rolled umbrella,

* Someone told me that the deep purple form originated on one of
the Greek islands, but they couldn't remember which.

and then bring it indoors and watch it open under a lamp. If you have the patience to watch for long enough, you will see this miracle happen.

If you have not yet got this iris in your garden and want to acquire it, you can plant it in March or April; but September is the best time for transplanting. It does not much like being split up and moved, so, whenever you acquire it, do make sure that it does not get too dry until it has had time to establish itself. After that, it will give you no trouble.

February 26, 1950

A dear near neighbour brought me a tussie-mussie this week. The dictionary defines tuzzy-muzzy, or tussie-mussie, as *a bunch or posy of flowers, a nosegay*, and then disobligingly adds that the word is obsolete. I refuse to regard it as obsolete. It is a charming word; I have always used it and shall continue to use it, whatever the great *Oxford Dictionary* may say; and shall now take my neighbour's tussie-mussie as a theme to show what ingenuity, taste, and knowledge can produce from a small garden even in February.

My neighbour has many difficulties to contend with. She is not young, she is into her seventh decade. She has no help in her house. Her garden is wind-swept, and the soil is a stiff Weald of Kent clay. (Only those who have tried to garden on Wealden clay can appreciate what that means.) A jobbing gardener from time to time is all that she commands. She does most of the work herself. Yet she manages to produce a bunch such as I will now describe to you.

It is composed of at least five different flowers, all perfectly chosen. She goes always for the best, which I am sure is the secret of good gardening: choose always the best of any variety you want to grow. Thus, in the bunch she brought me, the violets were *pink* violets, the sort called

Coeur d'Alsace, and the one *Iris Reticulata* she put in was
the sort called *Hercules,* which is redder than the familiar
purple and gold. The grape-hyacinths were the small sky-
blue *azureus,* which flowers earlier and is prettier than the
dark blue later sort. The crocus in her bunch was not the
common yellow, but had brown markings on its outside;
I think it may be *C. susianus* or it may be Moonlight, but
I forgot to ask her. The anemone that she put in must be
a freakishly early bloom of *Anemone St. Bavo,* amethyst
petals with an electric-blue centre. How wise she is
to grow *Anemone St. Bavo* instead of the coarser *Anemone
St. Brigid.*

The moral of this article, if any newspaper article may
have a moral, is that it just shows what you can do if you
put your mind to it. I have received many letters saying:
'Do tell us what we can do in a small garden.' My neighbour's tussie-mussie is the answer. She grows those exquisite things in a small, quarter-of-an-acre grassy space
under apple trees, and somehow produces a jewelled effect
rather like the foreground of Botticelli's *Primavera.* They
are all low and brilliant and tiny; and no more difficult to
grow than their more ordinary relations.

Some day I must write an article describing the way my
neighbour has designed her garden; and also, perhaps, what
she manages to do with her small, unheated greenhouse.
You would be surprised.

February 4, 1951

I notice that people become enraged over the names of
plants, and I don't wonder. I wish only that they would not
blame it on me. 'Why,' they write indignantly, 'why can't
you give us a good honest English name instead of all this
Latin?' Well, whenever there is an English name, I do give
it; I prefer it myself; I would much rather call a thing
Bouncing Bet than *Saponaria officinalis;* but when there is

no name in the vernacular, our common speech, what am I to do?

Instead of getting cross about it, we should do better to take an intelligent interest in discovering what lies behind these apparently appalling names. There is always a reason, and the best reason is that by using an international idiom, such as Latin, botanists and gardeners can understand one another all the world over. If I see that a plant is described as *azureus* I know instantly that it is blue, and so does my opposite number in Brazil, France, or Pakistan. If it is described as *azureus vernus*, I know that it is not only blue, but that it flowers in the spring. Then if you want to indicate what explorer first found it, you tack on, say, *Farreri*, or *Fortunei*, which we can all manage, or *Mloko-sewitchii*, which perhaps we can't.

There appear to be two principal grievances. I hope I have disposed of the first one, but I do suggest that some society such as the Royal Horticultural Society might supply an inexpensive alphabetical glossary for easy reference. If such a thing exists, I do not know of it. It would be a great convenience; we should all rush to look up *strobili-formis* or *quintuplinervius*, only to discover that it meant *shaped like a fir-cone*, and *five-veined* in the description of a leaf.

The second grievance concerns changes of botanical name. I admit that it is very puzzling to be brought up in our childhood to call lilac *lilac*, and syringa *syringa*, and now suddenly to be told in our middle-age that we must call lilac *syringa* and syringa *philadelphus*; but here again there is a good respect-worthy reason, in the attempt either to get back to the first names given by earlier botanists, or to define a new botanical classification, in the interest of accuracy and in the avoidance of confusion.

All the same, sentimentally, Bet may bounce as happily as she likes over my garden, and all her friends, too.

February 11, 1951

With the Festival of Britain approaching, many people will be thinking how to make their front gardens as attractive as possible for the passing motorist. An English village street, gay with flowers, can be as pretty a sight as anyone could wish to see; and, moreover, is not to be found elsewhere in just that way, thanks to our climate and to the Englishman's passion for gardening. Most of these small front gardens are already well furnished with beds, but it would be pleasant to feel that something more permanent was also being planted, to commemorate the Festival year, as things were planted to commemorate the Coronation in 1937.

Such permanent planting inevitably means trees or shrubs, both of which unfortunately have a habit of growing until they begin to obscure the light from the windows. Then the occupant of the house quite understandably prunes the poor thing back into a sort of mop head, when all its beauty is lost. A mop on top of a stick is very different from the loose, natural development of the mature plant smothered in flower or blossom. An ingenious way of getting out of this difficulty is to train the branches along post and wire, like an espalier apple or pear in an old kitchen garden. The flowering trees, by which I here mean the prunus, the pyrus, the Japanese cherries, the almonds, and all the other members of those lovely families, lend themselves very obligingly to such treatment, and I am sure prefer it to being hacked about and thwarted from what they want to do, which is to give as generously as they can of their load.

Have I made myself clear? No, I don't think I have. I often long to draw a little explanatory diagram, but I can't draw. So, without the aid of a diagram, may I suggest that you might run a row of flowering trees from your front gate to your front door, training them horizontally so that they will not obscure the light from your windows and yet will make a path of blossom from gate to door along our village streets.

It is not too late to plant now. You can plant anything between now and March.

Next Sunday I will write something about hedges of roses, fronting the road; another blandishment for our guests, and a pleasure for ourselves in the years after our guests have gone.

March

THERE are several kinds of Hellebore, but the two varieties usually seen in English gardens are more familiar under their prettier names of Christmas rose and Lenten rose, *Helleborus niger* and *Helleborus orientalis* respectively. Why the Christmas rose, which is white, should be called black in Latin I could not imagine until I discovered that the adjective referred to the root; but I still cannot imagine why people do not grow both these varieties more freely. They will fill up many an odd corner; their demands are few; and they will give flowers at a time of year when flowers are scarce.

As for their demands, they like a cool place, say a west aspect or a niche shaded by shrubs; a fairly heavy soil, and if it is moist so much the better; the one thing they will not stand is a poor sandy soil which gets dried out in the summer. They do not like being disturbed either, so plant them where you intend them to remain. If you buy plants you will have to wait a couple of years before they do anything very much about flowering, but once established they will improve steadily, especially if you give them an occasional mulch of compost, leaf-mould, or rotted manure.

It is, of course, cheaper to grow them from seed than to buy plants, and the seed germinates very readily if it is freshly harvested, say from the garden of a friend, in May or June.

Both the Christmas and the Lenten roses are true to their association with the calendar, which means that from

December to April the clumps of one or the other are in flower. The Christmas rose is ideal for picking, lasting for weeks indoors if you split the stems. Cover the clump with a hand-light, to avoid splashing with mud from heavy rain. The Lenten rose, alas, is unreliable as a cut flower; sometimes, by splitting the stems, it can be induced to hold up its lovely wine-coloured head for a few days, but at other times under the same treatment it flops mournfully after a few hours; I have never made out why. *

Those who share my taste for greenish flowers may like to grow the Corsican hellebore (*H. corsicus*), a tough and handsome plant whose tightly packed head of strangely livid blossoms will last either out of doors or in a bowl oᵢ water from early March to May. Before the flower buds open they look not unlike a bunch of Muscat grapes, but presently they open out flat, when they look like a miniature pale green water-lily, if you can imagine a water-lily about the size of a penny.

March 9, 1947

A pot of cyclamen is a favourite Christmas present, and very nice, too, but by this time (March) some recipients may be wondering what to do with it. Don't throw it away. It will repeat its beauty for you year after year if you treat it right. Treating it right means (1) keeping it moist so long as it continues to flower and to carry leaves; (2) letting it dry off by degrees after the last buds have opened and faded away; (3) keeping it, still in its pot, *unwatered*, in a frost-proof place during the remaining cold weeks, and then standing it out of doors, still unwatered, still in its pot, throughout the spring and early summer in a shady place; (4) starting it into life again in July or August. Starting it

* Subsequent information: plunge the tips of the stalks into nearly-boiling water.

into life again merely means giving it water again—very simple. It will then begin, quite quickly, to show new buds all over the corm; but to get the best out of it you ought then to re-pot it. It likes a rather loose soil, made up of fibrous loam, some gritty sand, and a handful of bonemeal, all mixed well together. *Do not bury the corm*; it should sit on top, three-quarters visible. Do not water too much at first, water more generously when autumn comes and you bring your pots into the shelter of a warm greenhouse if you have one; or on to a warm window-sill if you have not.

Do not ever, at any time, give too much water. If you do, your plant will very quickly notify you by turning its leaves yellow and by developing a soft rot in the stems of the flowers. There seem to be two schools of thought about the best way to water. Some growers say it is better to avoid overhead watering which may cause the corm to rot, and that it is better to stand the pot in a saucer or bowl with an inch or so of water, thus absorbing the moisture through the porous pot up into the roots, remembering to empty the water away when you think the plant has had enough. Other growers condemn the saucer idea.

A cottage friend of mine who grows some superb cyclamen on her kitchen window-sill tells me that her grandmother advised her to water them with weak tea. This may sound like an old wife's tale, but the tales of some old wives sometimes turn out to be right.

There are two kinds of cyclamen: the Persian, which is the one your friends give you, and which is not hardy, and the small, out-door one, a tiny edition of the big Persian, as hardy as a snowdrop. These little cyclamen are among the longest-lived of garden plants. A cyclamen corm will keep itself going for more years than its owner is likely to live. They have other advantages: (1) they will grow under trees, for they tolerate, and indeed enjoy, shade; (2) they do not object to a limy soil; (3) they will seed themselves and (4) they will take you round the calendar by a judicious planting of different sorts. *C. neapolitanum*, for instance, will precede its ivy-like leaves by its little pink flower in late autumn, white flowers if you get the variety *album*; *C. coum*, pink, white, or lilac, will flower from December to March; *C. ibericum* from February to the end of March; *C. balearicum* will then carry on, followed by *C. repandum*, which takes you into the summer; and, finally, *C. europæum* for the late summer and early autumn. Some botanists believe this to be a native; it was certainly recorded here in the reign of Queen Elizabeth, when, if beaten into little flat cakes, it was considered 'a good amorous medicine to make one in love.'

Anyone who grows the little cyclamen will have observed that they employ an unusual method of twiddling a kind of corkscrew, or coil, to project the seeds from the capsule when ready. One would imagine that the coil would go off with a ping, rather like the mainspring of a clock when one over-winds it, thus flinging the seeds far and wide, and this indeed was the theory put forward by many botanists. It would appear, however, that nothing of the kind happens, and that the seeds are gently deposited on the parent corm. Why, then, this elaborate apparatus of the coil, if it serves only to drop the seed on to a hard corm and not on to the soft receptive soil? It has been suggested, notably by Mr. A. T. Johnson, that this concentration of the seeds may be Nature's idea of providing a convenient little heap for some distributing agent to carry away, and he points out that ants may be seen, in later summer, hurrying off with the seeds until not one is left. I confess that I have never sat up with a cyclamen long enough to watch this curious phenomenon of the exploding capsule; and I still wonder how and why seedlings so obligingly appear in odd corners of the garden—never, I must add, very far away from the parent patch.

You may find some of them a little difficult to obtain now, but *C. europæum*, *coum*, and *neapolitanum* are still listed by nurserymen, and are the three varieties I would recommend for a start. So accommodating are they that you can plant them at almost any time, though ideally they should be planted when dormant, i.e. in June or July. Messrs. Barr & Sons, King Street, Covent Garden, London, W.C.2, have a good list.

March 6, 1950

Successful gardening is not necessarily a question of wealth. It is a question of love, taste, and knowledge. The neighbour about whom I was writing on page 35 possesses all these virtues, added to fingers so green that the water must surely turn emerald in the basin every time she washes her hands. There are two things I should like to describe to you in connection with my neighbour: one is the way she has designed her garden, and the other is the way she makes use of her small greenhouse.

Which shall I take first? The greenhouse, perhaps, since this is the time of the year when one can make the best use of a greenhouse for growing seeds and for producing a display of flowers. My neighbour does both, and does it in the most unconventional fashion. It would make any professional gardener laugh, and would send him away scratching his head with a lot to think over. She does the oddest things. She digs up clumps of violets from her outdoor garden and has them blooming exuberantly in pots, the small pink violet and the little almost-blue one; and as she takes the trouble to whitewash her pots, instead of leaving them to their normal hideous terra-cotta colour, you may imagine how the flowers gain in beauty as they pour over those blanched containers, white and clean as blancoed tennis-shoes. She digs up clumps of snowdrops and crocuses, and packs them into an ordinary pudding basin.

One end of the house is all flowers and colour; the side-stagings are devoted to seed boxes.

She has not many real wooden seed boxes. There are cardboard dress-boxes tied round with string to prevent them from disintegrating, and old Golden Syrup tins, and even some of those tall tins that once contained Slug-death, and some of those little square chip-baskets called punnets. I verily believe that she would use an old shoe if it came handy. In this curious assortment of receptacles an equally curious assortment of seedlings are coming up, green as a lawn, prolific as mustard-and-cress on a child's bit of flannel. There are cabbages and lettuces in some of them; rare lilies in others; and I noted a terrified little crop of auriculas scurrying up, as though afraid that they might be late for a pricking-out into the warm earth of May.

It all goes to show what you can do if you try, in gardening. There are such possibilities, not necessarily expensive.

I was half mistaken, by the way, in describing this greenhouse as unheated. It *is* unheated as a rule, but on a chilly evening when a threat of frost is in the air an electric tube underneath the staging can be turned on by means of a switch located in the kitchen. What could be simpler? No need to bother with a stoke-hole or paraffin radiators; no need to go out into the cold night. It is rather an extravagant method, but that it is clean and labour-saving cannot be denied.

March 12, 1950

This is going to be about designing a small garden. By a small garden I mean anything from half an acre to two acres. It is a big subject to tackle in so short an article. I can hope only to give a few general ideas.

The small garden may be a bungalow garden, or a council-house garden, or the garden round an old cottage, or the garden round a new house on a main bus route.

Whichever it is, the true gardener will wish to make the most of the patch of the planet Earth at his personal and particular command. In most cases his design will be dictated by the shape of his patch, and by the position of his dwelling-house in it: thus, he may feel compelled to have a straight path running from the front gate to the front door, and to arrange his flower-beds, his borders, and his bit of lawn accordingly, in which case his garden will look exactly like his next-door-neighbour's garden. What I would like to suggest is that a little ingenuity can vary the pattern.

I have three gardens in mind. One of them has been constructed in front of a small house facing the road. It has been turned into a landscape garden on a miniature scale. The path does not run straight from the front gate to the front door but wanders round sideways, and the middle part of the front garden is occupied by a deep pool surrounded by weeping willows and *Iris Sibirica*, reflecting their pale mauve and their deep purple into the water. Some Irish yews have also been planted; and they now reflect their images into the pool, duplicating themselves in the watery mirror and making this tiny garden look twice the size it is.

My next garden also faces a road, a main road. It would have been easy, and obvious, to turn this into a conventional sort of garden. But the owners have designed it cleverly: they have put it sideways to the house, so that the flower beds, which ought, in the conventional way, to be geometrically set along the house, are put in a surprising way alongside.

My third garden is the sort of garden I like best. It is a cottage-garden of the best sort, kept by a true gardener. This is a garden that slopes rather vaguely downhill towards Romney Marsh, with views of the Marsh beyond it. It is packed with flowers at all times of the year, so exquisitely arranged that they gain their full value wherever they are.

I remember specially a planting of the blue primrose mixed with the blue scilla round the base of a grey stone well-head, a perfectly-chosen combination.

March 19, 1950

Several correspondents have asked me to say something about that strangely coloured black and green flower commonly called *Iris tuberosa*, or the Snakeshead iris, which is to be found in florists' shops during March and April, sold in bunches, rather cheap. I like being asked these questions, because they come as a challenge to my own many failures in gardening and make me examine my conscience to see where I have gone wrong. I have certainly gone wrong over my *Iris tuberosa*. I planted it in rather too shady a place, under an apple tree, in a rich old soil, and I now see that it ought to be given the maximum of sun, in a gritty, well-drained soil, exposed to as much baking as our English summer will afford.

It should not be difficult to grow. The tuber will cost you from 4s. 6d. to 5s. 6d. a dozen, and it should increase itself if you put it in the right sort of place, dry, hot, and sunny. An Italian by origin, it grows wild in other parts of southern Europe, all indicating that it would enjoy conditions as near as we can get to the Mediterranean coast.

A wise precaution: mark its position in the garden by a stick or a ring of stones, because it disappears altogether during the summer, and thus is liable to get dug up by mistake.

This may sound rather dull, perhaps: but my researches into the history of *Iris tuberosa* did not prove dull in the least. It is an interesting plant, in both botanical and mythological terms. Botanically it is not a true iris at all. Its real name is *Hermodactylus tuberosus*, which being interpreted, means Finger of Hermes (Mercury), and *tuberosus*, of course, refers to the tuberous root-stock, which does indeed bear some resemblance to the fingers of the human hand. Having got thus far, I began to reflect on its familiar sobriquet, the Snakeshead, and to wonder whether the current explanation was correct in attributing the name to a fanciful likeness to the head of a snake. Perhaps, I thought, there may be a double meaning, for although the sombre sinister colouring and spiteful shape do suggest the spitting head of a reptile, it is also true that Mercury's winged wand, the *caduceus*, that swift and elegant symbol of the most roguish of all the minor gods, was twirled round by two interlaced serpents. Would it be possible, and even probable, I wondered, that the name might have a classical origin we never suspected? I like to think so. I like to think that the messenger of the gods, Hermes in Greece, Mercury in Rome, gave his symbol as the name to one of our messengers of spring.

March 26, 1950

We now approach the time of year when the thoughts of Man turn towards the pruning of his roses. Knives and secateurs are now at their sharpest. Brandishing these objects of destruction, battalions of professional and amateur gardeners advance, prepared to do their worst, as they have immemorially been taught. The word of command has gone out: 'Cut almost to the ground; cut down to the second or third bud; cut till nothing is left except a couple of inches sticking up. Be pitiless, be ruthless; prune for fine blooms, exhibition blooms, even if you don't intend to exhibit. Never mind about the appearance of your garden, or the natural alacrity of your roses. Snub them as hard as you can, even as Victorian parents snubbed their children.'

It rejoices me to see that different ideas are creeping in. The rose, even the hybrid Teas and the hybrid Perpetuals, is no longer to be regarded as a stunted dwarf, but as a wildly blossoming shrub. Let her grow up, even to three or four feet in height, and throw her head about as I believe that she was meant to. This truth first dawned upon me during the war, when as a Land Army representative I had occasion to visit many small gardens in pursuit of owners who had been called away. Their gardens were turning into a sad disorder of weeds, but the roses reared themselves up, superb and proud, just because they had not been interfered with for two, three, four, five years. Then in the well-kept garden of a friend I saw similar rose bushes which, she assured me, had scarcely been touched since she planted them thirty years ago. She had merely snipped the tips; had taken out the dead wood and the weak growth; and for the rest had left them to their will. The result was lavish and surprising.

My liking for gardens to be lavish is an inherent part of my garden philosophy. I like generosity wherever I find it, whether in gardens or elsewhere. I hate to see things scrimp and scrubby. Even the smallest garden can be prodigal within its own limitations, and I would now suggest that you should try the experiment of NOT slaughtering your roses down to almost ground level, at least for this year; and see what happens.

I know that I have touched only the outskirts of this controversial subject. There is so much to be said, and so many different types of rose to deal with, that it all becomes confused and confusing. Everyone agrees that the hybrid Musk and the species roses are better without the knife, but no doubt the new unorthodoxy about the hybrid Teas will evoke screams of protest. I am prepared to admit that it might not suit them all. The only thing is to be bold; try the experiment; and find out.

April

April 6, 1947

I MUST start with a warning not to despair about plants apparently killed by the frosts, ice-rain, east winds, and other afflictions they have had to suffer. (Written in April 1947). They may look dead now, but their powers of revival are astonishing. You may have to cut some shrubs down to ground level, but my recommendation would be not to dig anything up rashly until you are quite, quite certain that it has no intention of putting out green shoots again. This certitude may not come until the summer is well advanced. I remember the agreeable surprises we got after the cruel winter of 1940.

All garden work has been so much delayed that many people will have to rely on generous sowings of annuals this year for extra colour. If you have not time to spare for the ideal method of growing them in boxes and then planting them out, you still have a large choice of those which may be sown straight into the ground. A finely broken soil; sow thinly, not too deep; thin out remorselessly, for most annuals will fill a space from a foot to two feet wide if given the chance, looking sturdy and bushy instead of drawn and spindly; and remember that it is far more effective to sow large patches of a few varieties than small patches of many. What you sow must depend upon your personal taste and the colouring you want. As a change from the usual jumble, pretty and gay though that may be, you might find it more original to concentrate on one colour. A combination of

Phacelia, Nigella (love-in-the-mist), *Nemophila, Asperula azurea*, would give a brilliant blue effect, especially if massed in front of delphiniums. Coreopsis, Eschscholtzia, Calendula Orange King and Lemon Queen, Nemesia yellow and orange (not quite hardy) would lie like a pool of sunlight. Mauve and purple stocks, Alyssum Lilac Queen, mauve Candytuft, mauve Godetia, Clarkia Purple Prince, Petunias (not quite hardy), make a sumptuous association. These are only a few suggestions, just enough, I hope, to indicate what scope there is for ingenuity.

April 2, 1950
A very pleasing little shrub or small tree, not often seen in gardens, has been in flower since the middle of March. It is not at all showy, and most people would pass it by without noticing, unless they happened to catch a whiff of the scent. It is pure vanilla.
This is *Azara microphylla*.
I would hesitate to recommend it except to gardeners who want something their neighbour probably hasn't got; but, after all, it is for those gardeners that I write these articles. Gardeners who want something different from the usual, and yet something easy to grow. *Azara microphylla* is quite easy to grow. It is an evergreen; it has neat little shiny leaves that look as though they had been varnished; and it has this tiny yellow flower which is now spreading its scent over my writing table and into the whole of my room. I sit and sniff. Wafts of vanilla come to me as I write.
Azara microphylla is a native of Chile, in South America. Some authorities say that it is not hardy here in Britain except in the favoured climate of Devon or Cornwall. I don't believe this. I have got it thriving where I live in Kent, and I have seen a twenty-foot-high tree of it in the rather colder climate of Gloucestershire. So I would say: plant it and risk it.
It likes to be planted in leaf-mould. It would do well trained

on to a wall with a north, or east, or west aspect; by which
I mean that the early morning sun would not get at it after
a frosty night. This is always an important point to remember when you are planting things affected by frost and by
the warm morning sun which comes as too great a shock
after the chill of the night. Plants must be let down gently.
The transition must not be too quick.

Another shrub I would like to recommend is *Osmanthus
Delavayi*. This, also, like the *Azara microphylla*, has dark
green box-like leaves and a scented flower, white, not yellow.
It flowers in March and April, and you can cut it and cut it,
and the more you cut it the better it grows. It is well worth
the attention of gardeners who want something away from
the ordinary.

How charming they are, and how subtle, these early
spring-flowering shrubs! We are all well accustomed to
watching the daffodils come up year by year in the orchards;
but how few of us think of fanning our English air with
vanilla from *Azara microphylla* or with the scent of the
Osmanthus which Father Delavay found in Yunnan some
sixty years ago.

April 9, 1950

For once, instead of giving advice, may I ask for it? How
does one protect the choicer sorts of primroses from the
attack of sparrows? Has any reader of these articles a
sovereign remedy against this naughty, wanton, wild
destruction? Short of putting automatic cartridges amongst
my primroses, I have done everything I can think of. I have
made a sort of cat's cradle of strong black thread, pegged
down in the hope that the birds would catch their nasty
little claws in it as they alighted and thus be frightened
and discouraged. It doesn't work. The sparrows don't
seem to mind. I can suppose only that they crawl underneath the threads and nip the flowers off, scattering the buds

and the heads all over the ground at dawn before I have got up in the morning.

This is a real S.O.S. I have quite a collection of uncommon primroses, Jack-in-the-Green, Madame Pompadour, Cloth-of-Gold, and so on, but what is the good of that if the sparrows take them all? I would try not to grudge them their fun if it was of any benefit to them, but it isn't. They are mischievous hooligans who destroy for the sake of destruction.

Some of these old primroses are very charming and there are signs that, like several other old-fashioned flowers, they are coming back into favour. Unfortunately they are neither easy to obtain nor to grow. Sometimes one sees a happy clump of the double white or the double purple in a cottage garden, but then it is a truism that things will flourish without any attention at all in a cottage garden, when all the skill and science of the professional well-instructed gardener leads only to the petering-out of the last miserable sickly survivor. Still, the doubles do not appear to be so choosy, and a half-shady corner with plenty of leaf-mould should suit them. They associate very gladly with their relations the Auriculas, or with the Hepaticas (a kind of anemone), and they are all, I think, plants for an intimate recess where their low beauty may be studied apart from the flauntings of their spring contemporaries such as the daffodils. They need to be observed in the small secret of their chosen shade.

This is all very well, but what am I to do about the sparrows?

* * *

The Pasque-flower, *Anemone pulsatilla*, is blooming just now, for Easter as its name indicates. This is a native of our Downs, getting rare in its wild state, but still cultivated in gardens. It is a soft and lovely thing, pale lilac in colour

with a silvery floss-silk surround: and it can now be obtained
also in a rosy-pink colouring, which mixes and merges
most exquisitely with the original mauve of the native.
Maurice Prichard & Sons, Riverslea Nurseries,Christchurch,
Hampshire, specialize in these. There is also a white form.
It is easy to grow anywhere, though as a native of the chalk
hills it appreciates a bed of limy rubble in the sun.

The sparrows so far, touch wood, have left it alone.

April 16, 1950

When I was small I had a book called *Flowers that do not
disappoint*. They nearly all did, but that was probably my
fault so far as the annuals were concerned. Hardy annuals
should not disappoint, and there is still time to sow them in
April, so useful for filling bare patches or for making a
display in the window-boxes of town houses.

The charm of annuals is their light gaiety, as though they
must make the most of their brief lives to be frivolous and
pleasure-giving. They have no time to be austere or glum.
They must always be youthful, because they have no time
to grow old. And so their colours are bright, and their
foliage airy, and their only morality is to be as cheerful as
possible, and to leave as much seed as they can behind them
for their progeny to continue in the same tradition. This,
of course, is the one thing you must not let them do: all
seeding heads must ruthlessly be snipped off if you want to
prolong the exuberance of flowers.

So much advice has been given about sowing annuals
that it is perhaps unnecessary to repeat it in too much detail.
The ground should be well dug, but, generally speaking, not
over enriched, unless it is very poor. It should be broken
down into a fine surface tilth. The piece of advice that people
never take is: sow thinly and thin out remorselessly; but if
ever you have noticed a solitary plant growing with ample
space all round it you will be better disposed to listen. The

smaller the seed the shallower it should be sown, and it is better to sprinkle some fine soil over your sowings than to attempt to rake them in, a method which usually results in an uneven distribution. Look out for slugs. Put twiggy sticks among those seedlings that will eventually grow tall enough to need staking.

In a short article like this it is impossible to give an exhaustive list, but I might single out a few annuals that are less commonly grown than the usual clarkias, godetias, and so on. To take one of the tiniest first, I am very fond of *Leptosiphon*; only three inches in height, but very varied in colour, it is charming as an edging, or among stones, or in paving. It likes full sun. *Linaria* associates well with it, being several inches taller, but of the same delicate character, as the name *Fairy Bouquet* will suggest. *Phacelia campanularia*, nine inches, sown in large patches, will quickly make a mat of gentian-blue.

Among the stronger colours, *Coreopsis Crimson King* is a brilliant bronze dwarf. *Dimorphotheca aurantiaca*, the orange South African daisy, looks like a patch of sunlight on the ground (but shuts itself up when the sun goes in); and among the calendulas there is a strain called by the repulsive name of *Art Shades*, which throws a variety of pretty colours in apricot, buff, and straw, less violent than the old *Orange King*. A study of a seedsman's catalogue will give many suggestions, and there is also a very useful book, *Annuals* by Roy Hay, published by the Bodley Head at 12s. 6d.

April 23, 1950

A very pretty, clean little tree which has been in flower since the middle of this month (April) is the golden-barked Manchurian cherry, *Prunus Maackii*. With its pale green leaves and masses of tiny white flowers, it makes a change from the innumerable pinks and reds of the flowering trees one now sees in most gardens. I called it a little tree, because

mine is not very old yet, but I believe that eventually it will
grow to a height of forty feet. It must then be a lovely sight.

* * *

My thanks to all those who have written about remedies
against the attack of sparrows on primroses. For the benefit
of other sufferers, of whom there appear to be many, I
append a list of recommendations, which of course would
apply equally to attacks on other flowers, such as the yellow
crocus, a particular victim. Pepper seems to be the favourite
deterrent, though rather an expensive one; but dry mustard,
flowers of sulphur, Keating's powder, soot, powdered
naphthalene, quassia, soft soap, paraffin-and-water, saffron,
Jeyes' fluid, Izal, and basic slag are all mentioned. Earthen-
ware saucers sunk into the ground and filled with water
find great favour. Wire pea-guards (to be removed daily
after breakfast), wire netting to be bent into the shape of a
mob-cap over each plant, fish-netting, the old nursery fire-
guard, old hair-nets, sprigs of holly, and 'an ordinary dark
glass bottle on the ground,' have all been found helpful. Some
handfuls of confetti have also been found to do the trick.

Among things to dangle, I am advised to use Glitter-
bangs, tin foil, potatoes stuck with pheasants' feathers,
pieces of bright blue paper, a bell, and the coloured tops of
T.T. milk bottles. I am most grateful to the gentleman who
sent me a regular necklace of these. Among the unkinder
remedies I find mouse-traps, bright unbreakable beads for
the sparrows to chip their beaks upon, 'the body of a
sparrow on a little gibbet,' and 'a masterful young cat.'
It seems, however, that an old fur among the plants will
take the place of real cats, and that a pair of white china dogs
has proved very efficacious. A palisade of wooden pipe-
lighters is advised, also of bits of looking-glass or of old
gramophone records, splintered, 'preferably Bing Crosby.'

One humanitarian advocates a Sparrow Corner where the offenders may disport themselves in sand-boxes and bird-baths, and may amuse themselves with the sorrel, spinach and Sweet William, that you will have provided for them; but not all the sufferers are humanitarians, and in cases of great exasperation a shot-gun or a catapult may be brought into action.

Kindest of all, perhaps, is the recommendation to try Christian Science, to which it would appear that our feathered enemies are most susceptible.

I have left to the last the question of cotton. Apparently I went wrong in using strong black thread. I ought to have used thin cotton, of the 50 variety, and not thread at all. Even *blue* cotton would have been better. I apologize. And now you can take your choice.

April 30, 1950

The season for flower shows is now in full swing, and soon the Chelsea Show will open for four days. But beware. On that first day it will be open to Fellows only, so if you are not a Fellow of the Royal Horticultural Society you will not be able to get in. It is no use hoping to borrow a Fellow's ticket, because on this occasion they are not transferable. On the second day the entrance will cost you 10s., and on the subsequent days, which are cheaper, the crowd will be greater and many of the exhibits will begin to look sorry for themselves after all that time in a hot tent.

You will by now have perceived the moral of these remarks, which is to join the R.H.S. without delay. The R.H.S. has not asked me to say this, and will probably be surprised by so gratuitous an advertisement, should ever it come to its attention, but I truly feel that the advantages of Fellowship are wide enough to justify me in pointing them out. Some readers of *The Observer*, which, as I well know from my correspondence, finds its way all over the British

Isles and elsewhere, may protest that flower shows held in
London are not of much interest to them. I sympathize.
It is irritating to be told about things you cannot yourself
enjoy, unless you have a very altruistic nature indeed. So
let me give a list of other advantages.

You receive a free copy of the monthly R.H.S. journal,
which in itself is worth the whole subscription. You have
the right of free entrance to the R.H.S. gardens at Wisley,
Surrey, and also to the fortnightly shows at the Society's
halls in Vincent Square, London, S.W. If you cannot avail
yourself of this privilege you can lend your ticket to a friend.
You have the right to exhibit any plant or plants of interest
at these shows, including Chelsea. And, finally, you have a
share, free, in the annual distribution of seeds from the
Wisley gardens, a share which is doubled if you live more
than thirty miles from London. A list will be sent you
from which to make your choice.

All particulars can be obtained from the Secretary, R.H.S.,
Vincent Square, London, S.W.

*   *   *

The Balsam poplar has now unfolded its very sticky leaf-
buds and is scenting the air. It surprises me that this
deliciously scented tree should not be more widely grown.
It is not too large for even a small garden, and if only our
road planners and village beautifiers would plant it in
avenues along our new roads, or in clumps round our old
village greens, every motorist would surely stop with an
inquiring sniff. Smells are as difficult to describe as colours,
but I should describe this one as a sweet, strong resin,
powerful enough to reach for yards around in the open air
and almost too strong to put in a vase in your room.

Do not allow yourself to be fobbed off, as I foolishly was,
by anyone telling you that *Populus candicans* is as good as

Populus balsamifera. It isn't. You must insist on getting
P. balsamifera, alternately known as *tacamahac,* which I
take to be a Red Indian name, for the tree is a native of the
United States and Canada.

  P. trichocarpa is also said to be very powerfully scented.
If you can get cuttings from a friend's garden it will save
your pocket, for all poplars root very readily from cuttings
and will even throw out white worm-like roots in a glass of
water. Like all poplars, the balsam-scented tribe grows very
rapidly.

May

May 1948

BY the time this article appears the lilac should be in flower. It is not called lilac now by the experts: it is called syringa; and what we used to call syringa is now called philadelphus. All very confusing, so let us incorrectly retain the old names for the moment, when everyone will know what I mean.

Lilac (or laylock, if you prefer) is one of the few old favourites which has been definitely improved in recent years. Frankly, the pale mauve type was a washy thing. The newer sorts have gained in colour, size, and scent. I suppose that everyone is by now familiar with the earlier improvements: *Souvenir de Louis Spath*, and *Charles Joly*, both dark red; or *Charles X*, deep purple; or *Madame Lemoine*, double white; none of which is easy to beat. But not everyone, I find, is familiar with the more recent hybrids, carrying truly noble plumes of immense weight: *Réaumur*, dark red; *President Poincaré* and *Pasteur*, both claret; *Congo*, very dark reddish-purple; *Jeanne d'Arc*, double white; *Mme F. Morel*, mauvish pink; *Maréchal Foch*, red.

Any lilac is 'easy': they do not object to lime, in fact they like it; they need no pruning, though it is most advantageous to cut off the faded flowers, *this is really important*; they are perfectly hardy; and very long-lived unless they suddenly die back, which sometimes happens. Few plants could give you more for 8s. 6d. or half a guinea. Of course they repay rich cultivation; most plants do. And they like the sun.

The old syringa or Mock Orange, is another easy-going shrub, too often forgotten. Personally I like the early, very sweet-scented species, called *coronarius*, found in most old gardens; but *Virginal*, with double flowers, is a lovely cool green-and-white sight in midsummer; and so are *Belle Etoile* and *purpureo-maculatus*, both blotched with maroon in the centre. *Grandiflorus* is the one with big single white flowers, very decorative but entirely scentless, which may be a recommendation for people who do not like heavily-scented flowers in their rooms. By the way, if you strip all the leaves from cut branches of syringa they will last far longer, besides gaining in beauty. Try. And smash the woody stems with a hammer.

*   *   *

I end with a counsel and with a warning. *Counsel:* try to see plants in bloom during the coming months, either in private gardens open to the public—and there are many, my own garden, for instance, is open every day until the end of October—or at shows, or in nursery gardens, or in gardens such as Kew and the Royal Horticultural Society's place at Wisley. There is no better way of judging what plants really look like and what really appeals to you. *Warning:* this applies to slug-bait. Whatever you use, keep it away from dogs and cats, either by mixing it with tea-leaves or by tilting something like a tile or a piece of glass over it. It is wise to be on the safe side.

May 9, 1948
Agreeable incidents do continue to occur from time to time, even in 1948; and there still seem to be days when things marvellously go right instead of wrong, rarities to be recorded with gratitude before they can be forgotten.
Such a day, culminating in such an incident, was given

to me recently. I had had occasion to drive across ten miles of Kent, through the orchard country. The apple-blossom was not yet fully out; and it was still in that fugitive precious stage of being more of a promise than a fulfilment. Apple-blossom too quickly becomes overblown, whereas its true character is to be as tightly youthful as an eighteen-year-old poet. There they were, the closed buds just flushing pink, making a faintly roseate haze over the old trees grey with age; closed buds of youth graciously blushing as youth must blush in the presence of age, knowing very well that within a few months they themselves would turn into the apples of autumnal fruit.

But if the apple-blossom was no more than a pink veil thrown over the orchards, the cherry was at its most magnificent. Never had it looked more lavish than this year (1948), nor so white, so candidly white. This heavy whiteness of the cherry, always enhanced by the contrasting blackness of the branches, was on this particular afternoon deepened—if white may be said to deepen—by a pewter-grey sky of storm as a backcloth; and I thought, not for the first time, how perfectly married were these two effects of April: the dazzling blossom and the peculiarly lurid heaven which is only half a menace. Only half, for however wrathful it may pretend to be overhead, there are gleams of light round the edges, with lances of sun striking a church tower somewhere in the landscape. It is not a true threat; it is a temporary threat, put on for its theatrical effect— Nature's original of that most strange and beautiful of man's new inventions, flood-lighting.

Enriched by these experiences I came home, expecting no further delight that day; but on arrival I saw a closed van at the front door. Having long awaited some spare parts to repair the boiler, dreary, yet necessary, I walked round to the back of the van, thinking how quickly utilitarian life returned to oust beauty, and with a sigh prepared to investigate some graceless assortment of ironmongery whose function would be incomprehensible to me. But there was no such thing. Instead, a smiling young man confronted me, saying he did not know if I would be interested, but he had brought these . . . and opened the van as he spoke.

'These' were giant pansies, thousands and thousands of them. The van's dark interior was a cavern of colour. Some royal hand had flung rugs of velvet over the stacks of wooden trays. Purples were there; and subtler colours than purple: bronze and greenish-yellow and claret and rose-red, all in their queer cat-faces of crumpled velvet. I stood amazed. What an imaginative young man, I thought, to hawk this giant strain round the countryside, selling his plants to any buyer. When I questioned him, he said, modestly, that he hoped people would not be able to resist them.

He was probably right, and I wish him good luck in his enterprise. As for those whose houses do not lie on his road, a packet of seed should serve the purpose, and by next spring the ground should appear as though spread with the most sumptuous carpet from Isfahan.

May 15, 1949

An unusual way of treating clematis is to grow it horizontally instead of vertically. For this, you need a kind of oblong trellis of bamboo sticks, supported at each of the four corners on four stout little posts, about two feet high from the ground; or a rectangle of rabbit wire or sheep wire will do equally well, besides proving more durable. The effect to be aimed at is a low, flat, open-work table top, under which you plant your plant, and allow it to grow up through. Every few days in the growing season, you will have to go round and weave the strands in and out of the wire or trellis, for clematis grows at an amazing rate, once it starts, and its instinct is to grow perpendicularly, not flatly:

but do this as gingerly as you can, for clematis seems to resent the touch of the human hand.

Does all this sound too complicated? It isn't really, and the reward is great. For one thing you will be able to gaze right down into the upturned face of the flower instead of having to crane your neck to observe the tangle of colour hanging perhaps ten or twenty feet above your head. The full beauty of the flower is thus exposed to you, in a way that it never is when you see it only from underneath. And for another thing, the clematis itself will get the benefit of shade on its roots, in this case its own shade, with its head in the sun, which is what all clematis enjoy.

The big-flowered Jackmanii type is the most suitable for growing like this, or the Patens group, because both these kinds have flat flowers. The well-known dark purple Jackmanii looks splendid, or its variety *rubra*. *Nelly Moser* is a pale mauve, with a pink stripe; *Gipsy Queen* a very deep purple.

The same idea could be extended to many other climbers, say Honeysuckle, or the annual Morning Glory, and even to the strong-growing kinds of rose. The hybrid perpetuals, such as *Frau Karl Druschki*, white, or *Ulrich Brunner*, cherry-red, or *Hugh Dickson*, dark red, or the old pink thornless rose, *Zéphyrine Drouhin* (hybrid Bourbon) will break out from every joint if bent over in this way or merely pegged down to the ground at the tip of the shoots. The extra crop of flowers you will thus obtain imposes rather a strain on the plant, so leave only three or four shoots and give a little encouragement with manure or compost.

May 29, 1949

In these somewhat scrappy notes I go, rightly or wrongly, on the assumption that my readers welcome suggestions for something which, though not difficult to grow, is a little out of the ordinary. This week I would therefore like to put in a plea for some tulips less usually seen than our old friends the Cottage or the Darwin. I know full well that tulips will be over by the time these words appear in print, but as all good gardeners keep a notebook for their autumn orders months ahead, I put forward these hints for your autumn list.

The Parrot or Dragon tulips are well named, for some of them really do suggest the more gaudy macaws in their colouring, and the jagged edges of their petals always remind me of the wyvern, that winged heraldic cousin of the dragon. I tried this comparison on a gardening friend, who stared at me blankly and said she couldn't think what I meant, and what was a wyvern anyhow? But still I think that one should look at flowers in an imaginative way, to squeeze the fullest enjoyment from them.

The pink *Fantasy*, with its apple-green feathering, is fairly common; *Red Champion* is a deeper version of *Fantasy*, a real cherry-red, opening to an enormous size, and heavily fringed; *Orange Favourite*, smudged with buttercup yellow and green, not quite so large; the *Blue Parrot*, which is not blue at all but a deep mauve, really the colour of blackberry fool (horticulturists sometimes have very queer ideas about naming colours); *Sunshine*, a golden yellow—all these are fun to grow, and no more expensive to buy than the ordinary tulip.

But there are other far more frenzied variations. *Gadelan* was the maddest-looking tulip I ever had in my garden. It was smeared with as many colours as a painter's palette after a good day's work—dark blue, dark red, purple, green, white—and as to size, it must have measured eight inches across when fully opened. This costs 1s. 3d. a bulb, so I got only three as an experiment, and abstained altogether from the *Black Parrot* at a guinea. *Gadelan* was enough, for the moment, to keep me satisfied and startled.

'Parrotting,' as it is called, is due to genetic change, i.e. a kind of sporting. It is not a disease.

May 7, 1950

Perhaps I should entitle this article 'In Your House,' or 'Your Garden in Your House,' because I want to write something about cut flowers, inspired by an interesting letter from a gentleman describing himself as a botanist and horticulturist who has carried out researches on this very subject. This is the time of the year when owners of gardens begin to pick more recklessly, with less dread of spoiling their outdoor show, but this pleasurable occupation does take a long time, and the busy woman wants to make her flowers last as long as possible.

'The cause of difficulties with cut flowers,' says my correspondent, 'lies in the entry of air into the water-tubes of the flower stems during the period between cutting the flowers and placing them in water.' To prevent such disappointment, he recommends that you should place your newly cut flowers in recently boiled water while it is still just above tepid, i.e. not hot enough to sting your hand but warm enough to give your fingers an agreeable sensation of warmth. Cut your flowers, he says, during dull, sunless hours; a recommendation that we have all found out for ourselves; but I wonder how many readers of this article are going to go wandering round with a kettle of recently boiled water? These things take time, and one has other things to do. Still, I shall try it.

My correspondent condemns as an old wives' tale the placing of aspirin tablets or copper coins in the water. He gives a slight approval to lumps of charcoal, in so far as they absorb air from the water. I suppose that we all have our theories, but this idea of air entering the stems is worth consideration. I pass it on to you.

*   *   *

I now return to the garden proper. Have you got *Viburnum Carlcephalum*? If not, please get it at once. It is a hybrid of *Viburnum Carlesii*, which we all know and grow, and it is a far better thing. Its head of flower is tighter and denser; its scent is stronger; and its habit is vigorous. My own plant is young and small; but I am told by people who have seen it growing fully developed that it makes a huge bush in course of time. It is one of the most exciting things I have grown for years past; not very exciting as to its colour, which is white flushed with pink in the bud, but most exciting as to its powerful scent.

It is flowering now, April–May, and is obtainable from Messrs. John Scott, The Royal Nurseries, Merriott, Somerset.

Halesia carolina, the snowdrop tree, is also just coming into flower. This is a very pretty flowering tree, seldom seen; it is hung with white, bell-shaped blossoms, among pale green leaves, all along the branches. It can be grown as a bush in the open, or trained against a wall. There is a better version of it called *Halesia monticola*, but if you cannot obtain this from your nurseryman *Halesia carolina* will do as well. Messrs. Hillier, of Winchester, however, list them both.

May 14, 1950

Some proverbs are piercingly true; some are not true at all; some are half true. One of the half-true ones is the one that says familiarity breeds contempt.

Contempt is the wrong word. What we really mean is that we take certain virtues for granted when we live with them day by day. Our appreciation becomes blunted, even as the beautifully sharp blade of the pruning-knife someone gave us as a Christmas present has become blunted by Easter. There are things we grow in our gardens and forget about, and then remember suddenly, as I have just remembered

the Sweet Woodruff, that meek, lowly, bright green native
of Britain, so easy to grow, so rapid in propagation—every
little bit of root will grow and extend itself—keeping weeds
down and making a bright green strip or patch wherever
you want it.

Sweet Woodruff is its pretty English name. *Asperula
odorata* is its Latin name. It is obtainable from The Herb
Farm, Seal, Sevenoaks.

You can use it in many ways. You can grow it where
other plants would not grow, in shade and even under
the drip of trees. You can grow it as a covering plant to
keep weeds away. Then, in the autumn, you can cut the
leaves and dry them and make them into sachets which
smell like new-mown grass and have the faculty of retaining
their scent for years.

It is not showy. Its little white flowers make no display,
but it is a useful carpeter for blank spaces, and it certainly
makes 'sweet bags' for hanging in the linen cupboard to
discourage the moth or to put under your pillow at night.
Take note that it has no scent until it is cut and dried, so do
not be disappointed if you walk beside it in the garden and
catch no puff of scent as you stroll. Which reminds me that
this month of May is the time to sow that small, dim-
coloured thing, *Matthiola bicornis*, the night-scented stock.
I have just sown half an ounce of it, which cost me no more
than 1s. 3d. all along the pathway at the foot of a yew hedge,
and now look forward to some warm evening when the pale
barn-owl is ranging over the orchard and the strong scent
of the little stock surprises me as I go. This is anticipating the
summer, when only recently snow lay upon the ground, but
this modest little annual is so easily forgotten that a prod of
reminder should not come amiss. If you mix the seed with
the seed of Virginian stock, you will get a little colour in the
daytime as well as the scent after dusk.

May 21, 1950

Snobbishness exists among gardeners, even as it exists among other sections of the community. The gardener's special brand consists in a refusal to grow plants which, of startling beauty in themselves, have become too trite to seem worthy of a place in any self-respecting gardener's garden.

Trite is a sharp, unkind little word. In the dictionary definition it means 'worn out by constant use; devoid of freshness or novelty; hackneyed, commonplace, stale.' I must agree that we all get tired of seeing certain plants all over the place—aubretia, for instance, being allowed to blanket every so-called rock garden; and the Virginia creeper, *Ampelopsis Veitchii*, glued to red-brick houses, where its colour swears horribly with the brick when it turns to flame in autumn. Yet, could we but behold either of these for the first time, we should shout in amazement.

It is too late to hope for such an experience, but I do suggest that much can be achieved by using these poor vulgarized plants in a different way and in the right place. There is, for instance, a big silver birch of my acquaintance into which a Virginia creeper has loosely clambered. When I first saw it I couldn't think what it was. Great swags and festoons of scarlet hung in the sunlight amongst the black and silver branches of the tree, gracefully and gloriously looping from bough to bough, like something (I imagine, perhaps incorrectly) in a tropical forest, or at any rate like a stained-glass window or like glasses of wine held up to the light. It convinced me once and for all that *Ampelopsis Veitchii* should be grown *transparently*, not plastered against a wall. Any tall old tree would serve the purpose, an ancient pear or apple, or a poplar, if you cannot command a silver birch; and I think the same advice would apply to many of the ornamental vines, such as *Vitis Coignettiae*, with its great shield-shaped leaves of pink and gold, or *Vitis purpurea*, whose name explains itself.

Aubretia has certainly been overdone, but I still maintain that this Rock-cress can be used with tact and advantage. Tact means that it should not be allowed to ramp too freely. Advantage means that it should be set against the background that suits it best. A grey wall or a white-washed wall, or grey paving-stones, all make a good background, especially if you avoid the insipid old pale mauve and choose only the best strains, such as *Cambria*, red; *Crimson Queen*; *Godstone*, deep purple; *Kelmscott Beauty*, a double red; *Vindictive*, violet-red. These can all be supplied by Robinson Gardens Ltd., Eltham, Kent.

Aubretia will not always come true from seed, but cuttings will come true, and on the whole I find that they do not revert. Even if they do hybridize amongst themselves, you may get an interesting novelty peculiar to your own garden, which is the ambition of every true gardener.

May 28, 1950

The roses are coming out, and I hope everybody will take the opportunity of seeing as many of the *old* roses as possible. They may roughly be described as roses which should be grown as shrubs; that is, allowed to ramp away into big bushes, and allowed also to travel about underground if they are on their own roots and come up in fine carelessness some yards from the parent plant. It is impossible in so short an article to give an adequate list, and even more impossible to indicate their charm, usefulness, and beauty, but there are gardens in which they may be seen and nurserymen from whom they may be obtained. (One garden where a large collection may be seen is Hidcote Manor, in Gloucestershire, near Broadway and Chipping Campden; for times of opening, which are several days a week, consult the National Trust, 42 Queen Anne's Gate, London, S.W.1. I put this in for the benefit of readers who live in that part of the country; and must add that, apart from its old roses, it is, perhaps, the loveliest garden in the west of England.*

The old roses are a wide subject to embark on. You have to consider the Gallicas, the Damasks, the Centifolias or Cabbage, the Musks, the China, the Rose of Provins . . . all more romantic the one than the other. Take this phrase alone: 'In the twelfth century the dark red Gallic rose was cultivated by the Arabs in Spain with the tradition that it was brought from Persia in the seventh century.' That is pure poetry, surely, although it comes from a serious article in a serious journal and was not intended as anything but a mere statement of fact. It should send us with a new zest in pursuit of these once neglected beauties.

They are not neglected now; their virtues are recognized by professional gardeners and amateur gardeners alike. True, I have heard conventionally minded people remark that they like a rose to be a rose, by which they apparently mean an overblown pink, scarlet, or yellow object, desirable enough in itself, but lacking the subtlety to be found in some of these traditional roses which might well be picked off a medieval tapestry or a piece of Stuart needlework. Indeed, I think you should approach them as though they were textiles rather than flowers. The velvet vermilion of petals, the stamens of quivering gold, the slaty purple of *Cardinal Richelieu*, the loose dark red and gold of *Alain Blanchard*; I could go on for ever, but always I should come back to the idea of embroidery and of velvet and of the damask with which some of them share their name. They have a quality of their own; and from the gardener's point of view they give little trouble. No pruning to speak of, only a yearly removal of dead wood, and some strong stakes which seldom need renewing.

Have I pleaded in vain?

* See also a note on Hidcote Manor, reprinted on pages 221–31 of this book.

June

IN a recent article I referred briefly to the fact that many privately-owned gardens are now regularly thrown open to the public, and as this remark appears to have aroused some interest, I thought I might take this opportunity of amplifying it. I made it in a desire to urge keen gardeners to see as many gardens as possible, for the sake of the practical hints they might pick up there, apart from the pleasure they might gain. Nothing could be more useful to the amateur gardener than to observe other people's ideas, other people's successes, and other people's failures. At flower shows, such as the Chelsea Show, one knows that every plant has been specially grown, richly fed, and luxuriously prepared for the great moment, thus arousing our suspicion that its grower has sat up with it night after night, holding an umbrella over it when too heavy a thunder-shower threatened its petals; ready with a hot-water bottle lest a late frost should come with a cold breath; and in many ways cosseting it for the supreme peak of its life when it must be exposed to the gaze of the King and Queen and all the Royal Family at a morning preview, and then to the expert criticism of Fellows of the Royal Horticultural Society during the afternoon. A plant in a garden is different from this: it has had to take its chance. It has been ordinarily grown. It has suffered from our common climate even as we all have to suffer. Seeing it grow in somebody else's garden, we can assess its normal performance; we can then decide whether we ourselves like it and whether we dare to attempt it or not.

These gardens now open to our wandering inspection are widespread and various. They range over all the counties of England, Scotland, and Wales. I have been looking through the England and Wales list, which runs so generously into seventy pages. * What enticements are therein offered! Who could resist the desire to penetrate without delay into precincts with such romantic names as Hutton John, Heronden Eastry, Nether Lypiatt, Bevington Lordship, St. John Jerusalem, Castle Drogo, The House in the Wood, or Flower Lilies? All poetry is there, suggestive and evocative. One could go and sit in those gardens on a summer evening, and imagine what one's own garden (and one's life) might be. And again, who could fail to respond to the magic of an invitation to 'Magna Carta Island, until dusk,' or to a garden mysteriously named The Isle of Thorns?

Nor is this all. At Tinker's Corner, for instance, you are offered tea *and music*; Bickleigh Castle provides floodlighting and a moated Saxon chapel, modestly adding '*romantic interest,*'which one can well believe. Little Whyley Hall somewhat startlingly tenders not only cups of tea but big-game herds. You can see Shelley's birthplace and Rudyard Kipling's house. You will be given 'strawberries if ripe' at Kempsons in June. At Old Westwell you can see fur rabbits; peach blossom, topiary, and rare shrubs are elsewhere suggested for your enjoyment. And if you like to see how Royalty lives, you can go to Sandringham on any Wednesday during June, July, and September.

These are no more than random pickings out of an immense bran-pie. Anyone who wants the complete list can get it from the Organizing Secretary, National Gardens Scheme, 57 Lower Belgrave Street, S.W.1, telephone Sloane 9948. You pay a shilling entrance fee, and all

* 93 pages in the 1951 list.

benefit goes to the Queen's Institute of District Nursing.
(*Note:* I should add that since this article appeared, the
Queen's Institute has come to an arrangement with the
National Trust, by which a percentage of the takings are
given to the National Trust towards the cost of such gardens
as are the property of the Trust.)

June 12, 1949

The rheumatic, the sufferers from lumbago, and the
merely elderly, would all be well advised to try a little
experiment in sink or trough gardening. By sink or trough
we mean either those old-fashioned stone sinks now rejected
in favour of glazed porcelain or aluminium; or the stone
drinking-troughs with which pigs and cattle were once
content before they had heard of concrete. Repudiated now
by man and beast, they can be picked up in a house-breaker's
yard for a few shillings; and, raised to hand-level on four
little piers of brick or stone, may provide in this their second
life a constant pleasure and interest to those keen gardeners
who for one reason or another can no longer stoop or dig,
but who still wish to fidget happily with their favourite
occupation.

Fidget is perhaps the right word, for this is indeed a
miniature form of gardening. The sink-gardener is like a
jeweller working in precious stones. He makes his designs,
trying experiments which he can alter when they fail to
satisfy him, if he had the wisdom to keep a few pots in
reserve. Out comes the offending colour, and in goes the
befitting colour, neatly dropped in without any root
disturbance.

Choose as deep a trough as possible, to get the maximum
depth of soil. It must have a hole for drainage; and crocks
spread over the whole bottom for the same purpose. The
soil should be a mixture of fibrous loam, leaf-mould, sharp
silver sand, and very finely broken-up bits of old flower-pots.

On top of this gritty bed you then arrange rocks or even flat stones. No one can dictate to you how to dispose your rocks, for this will be according to each person's fancy, but one can at least make some suggestions about what to plant. It is very important to keep everything to the right scale. Here is a short list of things which should do well: *Thymus serpyllum* for carpeting; *saxifrages* of the Kabschia or the encrusted kind; the tiny Alpine forget-me-not, *Myosotis rupicola*; the tiny Alpine poppy; *Bellis Dresden China*, a very bright pink little daisy; *Erinus alpinus*, pink; *Veronica Allionii*, violet spikes; *Allium cyaneum*, a five-inch high blue garlic; and even the midget roses, *Roulettii* and *Oakington Ruby*; and the innumerable bulbs such as the early species crocuses (*Sieberi*, *Tomasianus*), and the early species tulips such as *linifolia*, bright red, or *dasystemon*, green and grey; or *orphanidea*, bronze; and scillas and chionodoxas and grape hyacinths . . . the list would be endless, had I the space. Not having the space, I must leave readers to their imagination. There is plenty of scope.

June 26, 1949

I am no blind believer in the 'improved' modern flower: I don't like delphiniums with stalks like tree-trunks; I don't like roses with no scent and a miserable constitution; but for the Russell lupins and the bearded irises one must make an exception. Everyone knows, and grows, the lupins; not everyone, I think, has yet realized the extreme beauty of the irises. So as June is just the moment to see them in flower I thought I would remind you of their beauty and their many advantages.

Their beauty is beyond dispute. No velvet can rival the richness of their falls; or, let us say, it is to velvet only that we may compare them. That is surely enough to claim for any flower? They suggest velvet, pansies, wine—anything you like, that possesses texture as well as colour.

(Wine, to a connoisseur, does possess texture.) Then, as to
their advantages, they are the easiest plants to grow. All
they ask is a well-drained, sunny place so that their rhizomes
may get the best possible baking; a scatter of lime in autumn
or in spring; and division every third year.

It may sound tiresome and laborious to dig up and divide
plants every third year, but in the case of the iris it is a
positive pleasure. It means that they increase so rapidly.
Relatively expensive to buy in the first instance, by the end
of the second or third year you have so large a clump from
a single rhizome that you can break them up, spread them
out, and even give them away. The best time to do this is
immediately after they have finished flowering—in other
words, at the end of June or beginning of July. Do not
bury the rhizome, but leave it showing above the ground;
this, again, is in order to let the sun reach it. The plant knows
this, however, and will push itself up even if you do cover it
over; but why give it that extra bit of trouble, when it
already has a great deal to do?

Colours must, of course, be left to the individual taste.
Those which we may roughly call reddish include *Cresset*,
Senlac, *Mrs. Valerie West*, *Maréchal Ney*, *Red Rover*
and *Cheerio*, which has nothing wrong with it except its
name. The wine-coloured ones include the magnificent
Betelgeuse, *Melchior* and *Ambassador*. *Cinnabar* is a rich
pansy-purple, very tall. All of these range in price from
1s. 6d. to 3s. 6d. There are also many fine yellows; but the
best thing is to obtain a catalogue from a nursery that
specializes in irises, say Messrs. Wallace, Tunbridge Wells;
or the Orpington Nursery, Orpington, Kent. The descriptions are not misleading, for no adjective could be too
extravagant. It is only you that will be.

June 4, 1950

I have a gardening dodge which I find very useful. It

concerns colour-schemes and plant-groupings. You know
how quickly one forgets what one's garden has looked like
during different weeks progressively throughout the year?
One makes a mental note, or even a written note, and then
the season changes and one forgets what one meant at the
time. One has written 'Plant something yellow near the
yellow tulips,' or 'Plant something tall behind the lupins,'
and then autumn comes and plants have died down, and
one scratches one's head trying to remember what on earth
one intended by that.

My system is more practical. I observe, for instance, a
great pink, lacy crinoline of the May-flowering tamarisk, of
which I put in two snippets years ago, and which now
spreads the exuberance of its petticoats twenty feet wide
over a neglected corner of the garden. What could I plant
near it to enhance its colour? It must, of course, be something which will flower at the same time. So I try effects,
picking flowers elsewhere, rather in the way that one makes
a flower arrangement in the house, sticking them into the
ground and then standing back to observe the harmony.
The dusky, rosy *Iris Senlac* is just the right colour: I must
split up my clumps as soon as they have finished flowering
and make a group of those near the tamarisk for next May.
The common pink columbine, almost a weed, would do
well for under-planting, or some pink pansies, *Crimson
Queen*, or the wine-red shades, as a carpet; and, for
something really noble, the giant fox-tail lily, *Eremurus
robustus*, eight to ten feet high. I cut, with reluctance,
one precious spike from a distant group, and stick it in;
it looks fine, like a cathedral spire flushed warm in the
sunset. Undoubtedly I should have some *eremuri* next
year with the plumy curtains of the tamarisk behind
them, but the *eremuri* are too expensive and one cannot
afford many of them.

This is just one example. One has the illusion of being an

artist painting a picture—putting in a dash of colour here, taking out another dash of colour there, until the whole composition is to one's liking, and at least one knows exactly what effect will be produced twelve months hence.

*   *   *

To conclude, may I recommend planting tamarisk? It is graceful, hardy, and no bother. You can control its size by hard pruning, if necessary, though for my own part I like to see it growing free. *T. pentandra*, sometimes called *T. hispidi aestivalis*, flowers in August and September; *T. tetrandra* is the one I have been writing about, and flowers in May. *T. anglica* flowers in late summer and does particularly well by the sea, where it can be used as a windbreak. They all strike easily from cuttings in autumn.

June 11, 1950

There is an evergreen argument about growing roses from cuttings. Nurserymen deprecate the method, for several obvious reasons preferring to bud their young scions on the various stocks of briar, e.g. a plant of saleable size is obtained in a shorter time; secondly, where a large supply of one variety is required the number of buds provided by the parent plant is probably larger than the number of cuttings which could be taken from it; thirdly, they contend (and they may be right) that the vigour of the wild stock improves the constitution of its fosterling.

Not being a nurseryman, I find it both cheap and amusing to raise a supply of roses for myself. Either I increase a variety which I have already got, or beg from a friend a cutting of something desirable which I lack. Thus, in a couple of years' time I have a sturdy little party growing away *on their own roots*; they have cost me nothing; and

I know that every fresh growth they throw up from the base is not one of those wicked suckers which, if overlooked, will eventually swamp the rose back to the stock of *Rosa canina* or *Rosa rugosa*. It will be a growth of the true rose, and can either be left where it is, or transplanted, or given away.

The procedure is simple. You take cuttings of well-ripened wood, with a heel at the base, and plant them *very firmly* in rows in some spare bit of ground, not where the sun will scorch them, and leave them there for a year, by which time they should be rooted and ready to move to their permanent quarters. The end of September or the beginning of October is the best time, I find, though some people advocate July as an alternative. The most important points to remember are that the wood must be well matured, i.e. not too soft, and that the cuttings must be trodden in so firmly that no wind can wobble them loose and no thaw after frost can heave them up. It is advisable to look them over whenever such dangers have occurred, and if necessary to tread them in again.

Do not expect 100 per cent success; some of them are bound to fail. It is a wise precaution to insert twice as many cuttings as you really need. It must also be remembered that some roses refuse to strike, for instance some of the Centifolias; but experience is the best guide, and, generally speaking, you should be rewarded with the smuggest self-satisfaction. A healthy rose-bush which you have yourself created is far more gratifying than one which arrives, ready-made, in return for a postal order. The experiment grows upon one after the first triumphs, and before long you may find yourself raising your own stock of flowering shrubs by the same method. Perhaps I should add that a hormone preparation such as Seradix A, obtainable from any sundriesman, is a great help in stimulating the formation of roots. Instructions are sent with the bottle.

June 18, 1950

Two years ago I had what I thought might be a bright
idea. It has turned out so bright, in both senses of the word,
that I must pass it on.

I had two small windswept beds (the size was eight yards
long by five yards wide each), divided by a path of paving
stones down the middle. I tried every sort of thing in them,
including a mad venture of hollyhocks, which, of course,
got flattened by the prevailing south-west wind, however
strongly we staked them. So then I decided I must have
something very low growing, which would not suffer from
the wind, and scrapped the hollyhocks, and dibbled in lots
and lots of thyme, and now have a sort of lawn which, while
it is densely flowering in purple and red, looks like a Persian
carpet laid flat on the ground out of doors. The bees think
that I have laid it for their especial benefit. It really is a
lovely sight; I do not want to boast, but I cannot help being
pleased with it; it is so seldom that one's experiments in
gardening are wholly successful.

The thyme we used was the cultivated or garden form
of the wild thyme, *Thymus serpyllum*, the form you
see creeping about between paving-stones on paths and
terraces. *Serpyllum* comes from the Latin *serpere*, to creep;
think of serpent; and in fact two old English names for the
wild thyme were serpille and serpolet. My serpolet lawn. . . .
The Romans believed its fragrance to be a remedy for
melancholia; and in later years, our own Elizabethan times,
it was thought to cure sciatica and whooping cough, headache, phrenzy, and lethargy.

We had the common purple sort, and the sort called
coccineus to give the redder patches, and also a little of the
white, which varied the pattern.

I have planted a few bulbs of small things in amongst the
thyme, to give some interest in the spring, when the thyme
is merely green. A patch of crocuses; a patch of the miniature

narcissus; a patch of the little pink cyclamen. It occurs to
me also that if you have not a flat bed to devote to a thyme-
lawn you could fill a sunny bank with it. Steep grass banks
are always awkward to mow, but the thyme would not need
any mowing, and it should revel in a sunny exposure with
the good drainage of a slope. You might plant some of the
rock-roses, or sun-roses, hybrids of *Helianthemum vulgare,*
amongst the thyme on a bank, though I would not do so
in a thyme-lawn, where it would spoil the effect of flatness.
These sun-roses can be obtained in a variety of brilliant
colours, ranging from pale buff and yellow to tomato pink
and deep red, and they flower for at least six weeks during
May and June.

I know I get too easily carried away by some new en-
thusiasm and by the ideas it suggests; but that is half the
fun of gardening. I will not apologize too humbly; so,
instead of boasting, I will make two practical recommendations as an end to this article. First, do plant *Abelia triflora.*
It flowers in June, grows to the size of what we used to call
Syringa, and is smothered in white, funnel-shaped flowers
with the strongest scent of Jasmine. Second, do plant
Cytisus Battandieri. This is a broom; and when it has
grown into a large tree it is hung with gold-yellow tassels
in June, with a peculiar scent. I could not think what the
scent was, till my kind host who had it growing in his
garden fixed it for me: 'It is the scent of pineapple mixed
with fruit salad.' He was right.

Cytisus Battandieri is supposed to be hardy, but I suspect
that in cold districts it would be safer to train it against a wall.

June 25, 1950

Spring and summer are well provided with flowering
shrubs, but it is a puzzle to know what to grow of a shrubby
nature for colour in the later months of July, August, and
September. There are the *hibiscus (Althea frutex),* some of

which are attractive with their hollyhock-like flowers, blue, pink, red, blush-pink, lavender, or white; and they have the advantage of living to a great age, for I remember seeing one in south-western France with a trunk the size of a young oak. Its owner assured me that it had been in her garden for over a hundred years. '*Mais bien sûr, madame, c'est mon arrière-grand-père qui l'a planté.*' It had been trained as a standard, with a great rounded head smothered in creamy flowers blotched with purple, giving the effect of an old-fashionable chintz; but, charming as the hibiscus can be, I suspect that it needs more sun than it usually gets here, if it is to flower as we should like. Perhaps I have been unlucky, although I did plant my hibiscuses—or should it be hibisci?—in the warmest, sunniest place.

Far more satisfactory, I find, are the hardy fuchsias. It is quite unnecessary to associate them only with Cornwall, Devon and the west coast of Scotland. Several varieties will flourish in any reasonably favourable county, and although they will probably be cut to the ground by frost in winter, there is no cause for alarm, for they will spring up again from the base in time to flower generously in midsummer. As an extra precaution, the central clump or crown can be covered with dry leaves, bracken, or soil drawn up to a depth of three or four inches; and in case of extremely hard weather an old sack can temporarily be thrown over them. Their arching sprays are graceful; I like the ecclesiastical effect of their red and purple amongst the dark green of their foliage; and, of course, when you have nothing else to do you can go round popping the buds.

The most familiar is probably *Fuchsia Magellanica Riccartoni*, which will flower from July to October. *F. gracilis* I like less; it is a spindly-looking thing, and *F. magellanica Thomsoni* is a better version of it. *F. Mrs. Popple*, cherry-red and violet; *Mme Cornelissan*, red and white; and *Margaret*, red and violet, are all to be recommended. They will cost you about 3s. 6d. a plant, and they like a sunny place in rather rich soil with good drainage. You can increase them by cuttings inserted under a hand-light or a frame in spring.

Other pretty and useful things for the late summer are the *Indigoferas*. They have pinkish, pea-like flowers dangling all along the tall, curving sprays. Like the fuchsias, they will probably get cut down in frosty weather, but this does not matter, because in any case you should prune them to the ground in April, when, like the fuchsias, they will shoot up again. They thrive at the foot of a south wall. There are several varieties, all desirable: *Gerardiana, Potaninii,* and *Pendula.*

Lespedeza Lieboldii (sometimes called *Desmodium pen-duliflorum*) resembles the indigoferas, and is a most graceful plant. Messrs. Hillier, of Winchester, list them.

July

July 20, 1947

THIS is a good moment to think of your future stock. Plants, and even seeds, are expensive to buy, but by raising your own nursery you can get plants by the thousand if you wish, for no cost beyond your own time and labour. It is well worth saving the seeds of annuals, biennials, and even perennials, either from your own garden or the gardens of friends who may have better varieties than you have. They must be quite ripe, and can be stored in little air-tight tins, such as the tins that typewriter ribbons come in, and sown in September when they will have time to make sturdy growth before the winter. Pansies, Indian pinks, columbines, foxglove, forget-me-not, primrose, polyanthus, anemones, lupins, and many other garden flowers can be thus harvested. Sow them thinly in drills on a finely pulverized seed-bed, and move them to their flowering quarters in the spring.

Remember that home-saved seeds will not necessarily come true, as the insects will have interfered with them. All the same, it is worth trying, and you might even get an interesting hybrid.

If you feel more ambitious you will be well advised to buy some packets of the improved varieties from a regular seedsman. Messrs. Sutton, of Reading, have some fine columbines. *Crimson Star, Scarlet and Gold, Longissima,* a magnificently long-spurred yellow, and *Azure Fairy,* a really lovely pale blue, will all surprise you if you have

hitherto grown only the old-fashioned kinds. The results
of a pinch of seed from the grand new delphiniums (obtainable from Messrs. Blackmore and Langdon of Bath),
if you can't cadge some from a friend, will put you out
of conceit with the sorts that have hitherto contented
you. Seeds of the hybrid *Alstroemeria*, or Peruvian lily,
will germinate freely, but as they are rather tricky to
transplant, I should advise you to sow them direct where
you want them eventually to grow; they like good drainage
and full sun, and the *Ligtu hybrids*, pink or buff-coloured, are
the sort to ask for; or *Alstroemeria haemantha* if you want
a flaming orange one.   Cover the seedlings with bracken,
or with the twiggy tops of old pea-sticks if you haven't
any bracken, for the first winter of their young life.

Lilies may also be raised from seed, instead of paying
half a crown or more for a single bulb. *Lilium regale* will
come up as thick as mustard and cress by this method; you
will have to wait two or possibly three years before the bulbs
come to flowering size, but think of the economy and of
the staggered crop that you can raise, if you sow even one
little row of seed every year.

Clematis will grow from seed, and so will broom; but as
both these hate being disturbed it is advisable to grow them
single in small pots, when they can be tipped out without
noticing that anything has happened.

Cuttings of many flowering shrubs such as ceanothus,
can be taken in July. Set them very firmly in a drill filled
with sharp sand, in the open in the shade. As with rose
cuttings, you should put in more than you need. A closed
frame or even a hand-light put over cuttings for the
first ten days or so will help them to strike, but they will
give quite good results without this. Remember the
hormone preparations recommended for rose cuttings on
p. 79; it will very greatly help any cutting to strike: simple
instructions are supplied with the bottle.

July 10, 1949

One learns a lot from visiting other people's gardens. One gets ideas. I got a lot of ideas from a famous garden I visited recently; so many, that I feel like a wine-glass spilling over; so many, that I cannot compress them all into this short article. So in this article I will concentrate only on the hedges I saw in that famous garden.

Hedges are always an important feature in any garden, however small, however large. Hedges are the things that cut off one section of the garden from another; they play an essential part in the general design. The only question is: What shall we plant for our hedges?

In this article I shall disregard the question of the flowering hedges; that is another subject, to which I hope to revert later on. I am here concerned only with the solid, useful hedge, deciduous or evergreen. We don't show nearly enough imagination about these. We still stick to such dull things as privet or *Lonicera nitida*, not realizing that we can make a muddle-of-a-hedge, which has a solidity and a character of its own.

In that famous garden I saw many different kinds of hedge, all planted in an imaginative mixture. There was yew mixed with box, and yew mixed with holly, and holly mixed with copper beech, and hornbeam mixed with ordinary beech, and one hedge mixed with five different sorts of plants in it—beech, holly, yew, box, and hornbeam, I think they were—but the most surprisingly sumptuous hedge, to my mind, was one made entirely of the copper beech.

We all know the copper beech as a tree; but few of us have thought of growing it as a hedge. Grown as a tree it has now acquired suburban associations. It works in with such things as *Prunus Pissardii*, very pretty in their way, but with which we are now only too familiar. Grown as a hedge, the copper beech acquires a completely different character. You would not believe the richness of its colouring. It has purple tinges in the depths of it, a sort of mulberry purple, and then Venetian red; and then the tips of the young shoots so bright a ruby as they catch the sunlight—oh, why, I cried to myself, don't we all plant even a short length of copper beech hedge? For my own part, I am certainly going to. *

July 24, 1949

There comes an awkward moment between June and September. Unless we go in for herbaceous borders, for which few of us can now afford the space or the time, if indeed we still had the taste for them, the garden is apt to go blank and green and colourless in these months of high summer. Annuals are our best hope, but annuals mean a good deal of trouble, especially in a dry season. So we turn to our faithful friends the flowering shrubs; and find very little.

Still, there are some. The misty blue ceanothus, *Gloire de Versailles*, which can be grown either as a bush or against a wall, is at its best in July. The deeper blue plumbago, *Ceratostigma Willmottiana*, flowers a little later, but sometimes coincides with the ceanothus, when they make a lovely sight planted in conjunction; and *Caryopteris mastacanthus* (or its variety *Clandonensis*), a low-growing shrub with grey leaves and powdery blue spikes, might join the group, with *Perowskia atriplicifolia* mixed in the foreground. A blue and silver corner, where only the names are vile.

Then there are the lavenders, so satisfactory at all seasons, but especially in this barren time of July and August. The old English lavender, *Lavandula spica*, is always a stand-by, whether you grow it as a hedge on either side of a path, or as a single bush. A particularly fine form is called *Twickle*

* See also pp. 226–7.

Purple, and *spica gigantea* is the tallest of all, but there are other forms of lavender which one doesn't see so often. There is the very dark purple, *atro-purpurea nana compacta*, and there are white lavenders and pink lavenders, in fact a great range of lavenders which are all very valuable in the garden at this time of the year. They are no more difficult to grow than our old friend the ordinary English lavender. Try them. The good gardener is the gardener who makes experiments.

They should all be cut back to the old wood after flowering to prevent them from getting straggly.

Then, if you like white flowers, as you should—for what can be more romantic than white flowers in the moon-drenched summer nights?—grow *Romneya Coulteri*, the big shrubby Californian poppy, and *Hoheria lanceolata*.* Not absolutely hardy, it resembles a syringa, which we are now taught to call *philadelphus*, but which we always knew as syringa in our youth. These syringas, or philadelphus, are also very useful shrubs for the late summer garden. You have *P. virginal*, with big white flowers, and *P. purpureo-maculatus*, white with a purple blotch in the centre; both scentless, alas, unlike the spring-flowering *P. coronarius*. Then there are the tree hollyhocks, or *Hibiscus syriacus*, sometimes listed as *Althea frutex*, which you can get with blue flowers, or claret coloured, or white, or mauve. They flower in August.

July 2, 1950

There are some moments when I feel pleased with my garden, and other moments when I despair. The pleased moments usually happen in spring, and last up to the middle of June. By that time all the freshness has gone off; every-thing has become heavy; everything has lost that adolescent

* See also pp. 92–3.

look, that look of astonishment at its own youth. The middle-
aged spread has begun.

It is then that the *Alstroemerias* come into their own.
Lumps of colour. . . . I have mentioned them before, I
know, but a reminder will do no harm. They are in flower
now, so this is the opportunity to go and see them, either in a
local nurseryman's plot, or in a private garden, or at a
flower show.The yellow Peruvian lily, *A. aurantiaca*, was and
is a common sight in cottage gardens and old herbaceous
borders, where it was regarded almost as a weed, but it has
been superseded by the far more beautiful *Ligtu* hybrids, in
varied colours of coral and buff, and by *A. haemantha*, a
brilliant orange. (Keep the orange away from the coral, for
they do not mix well together, and whoever it was who said
Nature made no mistakes in colour-harmony was either
colour-blind or a sentimentalist. Nature sometimes makes
the most hideous mistakes; and it is up to us gardeners to
control and correct them.)

The *Ligtu* hybrids of *Alstroemeria*, and also the orange
A. haemantha, can and should be grown from seed. You
sow the seed in February or March, where you intend the
plant to grow and flower. I am sure I am right in recommending this method. One reason is that the seed germinates very freely; another reason is that the roots of
Alstroemeria are extremely brittle, and thus are difficult to
transplant; and the third reason is that plants are expensive
to buy and may fail owing to the difficulty of transplanta-
tion. Therefore I say sow your own seed and wait for two
years before your clumps come to their fulfilment.

You could also sow one or two seeds in a pot, in those
cardboard pots which dissolve after they have been dropped
into the ground—this is perhaps the ideal method.

They demand full sun and good drainage, by which I
mean that they would not like any shade or a water-logged
soil. They are sun-lovers. They also demand staking, not

stiff staking, but a support of twiggy branches to hold them
up; otherwise they flop and snap and lose their beauty, lying
flat after a thunderstorm of rain or a sudden gale, such as
we get from time to time in our usually temperate country.
This is a counsel of caution. Prop up your *Alstroemerias*, if
you take my advice to grow them, by twiggy pea-sticks.

They are the perfect flower for cutting, lasting weeks in
water in the house.

The seedlings would like a little protection in winter
if there is a hard frost. Some bracken will do, scattered
over them. Once established, they are hardy enough to
withstand anything but a particularly bad winter. It is
only the young that are tender, needing a little love and
care.

July 9, 1950

A plant which I find always arouses a good deal of interest
in the summer here is *Humea elegans*. Visitors walk round
sniffing and saying: 'What is that curious smell of incense?
One might imagine oneself in an Italian cathedral instead
of an English garden.' They are quite right, for its other
name is the Incense Plant.

Eventually they track it down to a six- to eight-foot-tall
plant, with large, pointed dark green leaves and a branching
spike of feathery cedarwood-coloured flowers. It is neither
showy nor conspicuous, and nothing but the scent would
lead you to it among its more garish companions, such as
the delphiniums; yet it is graceful in its growth and well
deserves its adjective *elegans*. It makes its influence felt in
more subtle ways than by a great splash of colour. It steals
across the air as potently and pervasively as the sweet-briar on
a damp evening. I stick it into odd corners, where people
pass, or sit on benches, and pause for a moment before going
on their way.

A native of Australia, it is not hardy here, and must be

treated as a half-hardy biennial sown under glass in early summer, kept away from frost, and planted out in the late half of May or beginning of June. For this reason I cannot advise anyone to grow it who has not the advantage of a frost-proof greenhouse in which to raise it; but those fortunate gardeners who have even a tiny warmed greenhouse might well experiment with a few seeds in a pot: six seeds will give six plants, and six plants will be enough to scent the garden, especially if planted under the windows. It will tolerate half-shade, but the flower develops a richer colour in the sun; in the shade it dims off into exactly the same dingy tan as an old flower-pot. It likes a rich soil; it would love to be fed with liquid manure, and will grow all the better if you have time to give it this extra diet or a handful of Clay's fertiliser; but if you have not the time—and who has the time to attend to all these extra and special requirements?—it will do adequately well in ordinary garden soil, and will give you all the reward you can reasonably demand.

An additional attraction is that the flowering spike will last for at least a year indoors if you cut it off in autumn before the rain has come to sodden it. I kept some sprays of it in a vase for so long that I began to loathe the sight of the thing; it turned dusty long before it started to fade and die; it reminded me of those Everlasting Flowers, the *Helichrysums*, which are only too everlasting indeed.

You can save and ripen your own seed of it by cutting a spray or two and laying it out on sheets of paper in a sunny place. Do this before it has the chance to become blackened and sodden by autumnal rains.

I think I should add a word of caution. Some people appear to be allergic to *Humea elegans*, which brings them out in a rash which is anything but elegant. (Some primulas have this effect on some people.) It is a chancy danger which I would not wish any reader to incur owing to any fault of mine.

A visitor to my garden went off with a plant of it in a pot in his motor-car and not only did he arrive home scratching, but also his dog.

July 16, 1950

A beautiful thing in flower just now (July) is the Californian tree-poppy. It is not exactly a herbaceous plant; you can call it a sub-shrub if you like; whatever you call it will make no difference to its beauty.

With grey-green glaucous leaves, it produces its wide, loose, white-and-gold flowers on slender stems five or six feet in height. The petals are like crumpled tissue paper; the anthers quiver in a golden swarm at the centre. It is very lovely and delicate.

I don't mean delicate as to its constitution, except perhaps in very bleak districts. Once you get it established it will run about all over the place, being what is known as a root-runner, and may even come up in such unlikely and undesirable positions as the middle of a path. I know one which has wriggled its way under a brick wall and come up manfully on the other side. The initial difficulty is to get it established, because it hates being disturbed and transplanted, and the best way to cheat it of this reluctance is to grow it from root cuttings in pots. This will entail begging a root cutting from a friend or an obliging nurseryman. You can then tip it out of its pot into a complaisant hole in the place where you want it to grow, and hope that it will not notice what has happened to it. Plants, poor innocents, are easily deceived.

The Latin name of the tree-poppy is *Romneya*. There are two named sorts, *Romneya Coulteri* and *Romneya trichocalyx*. They are both much the same, except for a few botanical differences. *Coulteri* is perhaps the better.

It likes a sunny place and not too rich a soil. It will get

cut down in winter most likely, but this does not matter, because it will spring up again, and in any case it does not appear to flower on the old wood, so the previous season's growth is no loss. In fact, you will probably find it advisable to cut it down yourself in the spring, if the winter frosts have not already done it for you.

A good companion to the tree-poppy is the tall, twelve-foot shrub which keeps on changing its name. When I first knew and grew it, it called itself *Plagianthus Lyalli*. Now it prefers to call itself *Hoheria lanceolata*. Let it, for all I care. So far as I am concerned, it is the thing to grow behind the tree-poppy, which it will out-top and will complement with the same colouring of the pale green leaves and the smaller white flowers, in a candid white and green and gold bridal effect more suitable, one would think, to April than to July. Doubts have been cast upon its hardiness, but I have one here (in Kent) which has weathered a particularly draughty corner where, in optimistic ignorance, I planted it years ago. There is no denying, however, that it is happier with some shelter by a wall or a hedge.

July 23, 1950

The flowers of *Magnolia grandiflora* look like great white pigeons settling among dark leaves. This is an excellent plant for covering an ugly wall-space, being evergreen and fairly rapid of growth. It is not always easy to know what to put against a new red-brick wall; pinks and reds are apt to swear, and to intensify the already-too-hot colour; but the cool green of the magnolia's glossy leaves and the utter purity of its bloom make it a safe thing to put against any background, however trying. Besides, the flower in itself is of such splendid beauty. I have just been looking into the heart of one. The texture of the petals is of a dense cream; they should not be called white; they are ivory, if you can imagine ivory and cream stirred into a thick paste, with all the softness and smoothness of youthful human flesh; and the scent, reminiscent of lemon, was overpowering.

There is a theory that magnolias do best under the protection of a north or west wall, and this is true of the spring-flowering kinds, which are only too liable to damage from morning sunshine after a frosty night, when you may come out after breakfast to find nothing but a lamentable tatter of brown suède; but *grandiflora*, flowering in July and August, needs no such consideration. In fact, it seems to do better on a sunny exposure, judging by the two plants I have in my garden. I tried an experiment, as usual. One of them is against a shady west wall, and never carries more than half a dozen buds; the other, on a glaring southeast wall, normally carries twenty to thirty. The reason, clearly, is that the summer sun is necessary to ripen the wood on which the flowers will be borne. What they don't like is drought when they are young, i.e. before their roots have had time to go far in search of moisture; but as they will quickly indicate their disapproval by beginning to drop their yellowing leaves, you can be on your guard with a can of water, or several cans, from the rain-water butt.

Goliath is the best variety. Wires should be stretched along the wall on vine-eyes for convenience of future tying. This will save a lot of trouble in the long run, for the magnolia should eventually fill a space at least twenty feet wide by twenty feet high or more, reaching right up to the eaves of the house. The time may come when you reach out of your bedroom window to pick a great ghostly flower in the summer moonlight, and then you will be sorry if you find it has broken away from the wall and is fluttering on a loose branch, a half-captive pigeon trying desperately to escape.

July 30, 1950

Most of the *Verbascums* (mulleins) are useful in the summer garden. The Cotswold hybrids are by now well

known, *Cotswold Beauty*, *Cotswold Queen*, *Cotswold Gem*,
and other members of their family, variously named but all
looking as though clouds of small tawny or blushing moths
had alighted all the way up the stalk, to remain poised there
during the month of June. These hybrids are perennials,
and, moreover, will sow themselves generously, so that
once you have got them into your garden you need never
be without them. Their only disadvantage, so far as I can
see, is that they sometimes attract their own favourite brand
of caterpillar, which eats the leaves into a semblance of
lace-work; but he is very easily controlled, poor thing, by
a dusting of derris powder.

The *Verbascum* which has excited me this summer, however, is not one of the Cotswold family, but something quite
new to me in my ignorance, called *Verbascum Brusa*. Huge
grey-green leaves, heavily dusted with flour, throwing up
a spike six to seven feet tall, even more grey and woolly
than the leaves. It fascinated me to watch this spike growing
so rapidly, and to observe its pentagonal buds exploding one
by one into the yellow flowers. They came gradually: a
woolly grey bud one day, with a blunt yellow nose in the
middle of it, and a flat yellow flower the next. They went
on flowering for at least two months, through June and July.

I had planted my *Verbascum Brusa* against the dark
background of a yew hedge. They looked very handsome
there and they had the peculiar gift of inspiring all beholders
to attempt a definition of what they looked like. For my own
part, I had compared them to giant Roman candles, fire-
works, tethered to the ground, but somebody came along and
said they were like some strange sub-marine growth, waving
about; and somebody else said they ought to be growing in
a primeval landscape with a pterodactyl browsing amongst
them. Anyway, they had the art of arranging themselves into
grand curves, sweeping upwards, so that there was no
upright monotony about them, nor did they demand any

staking. I am assured by the nurseryman who introduced
V. Brusa into this country from Brusa in Anatolia that it
is a perennial, which I take leave to doubt. I think it is a
biennial, but I fancy that it will ripen its own seed so that
one should be able to harvest one's own supply for increase. *

Near them I had a group of *Onopordon Arabicum*, grown
from seed. It was too young this summer to throw up its
noble spikes of blue thistle-like flowers, but its large grey
leaves looked fine, with the same architectural quality as the
leaves of acanthus, and the background of the yew hedge
should be ideal for them.

* The verbascum proved itself very definitely to be a biennial.

August

August 17, 1947

I WRITE this note far from home, on a not unenviable expedition which involves wandering round other people's gardens. Most of them are still suffering from the neglect of the war years, from shortage of labour, and probably also shortage of funds, and only in a few cases the prosperity of herbaceous borders still flaunted under the long old walls. Such luxuries are not for the majority, so I turned to consider the flowering shrubs, those permanent mainstays which increase in value with every year, and demand less attention than any other plant in the garden.

It is generally recognized that the late summer shrubs are far less numerous than those of spring; nevertheless, some were prominent.

In some gardens the hydrangeas were making a great display, but they look their best in large clumps, I think, not as the single specimens for which a small garden has only room; and in any case they always remind me of coloured wigs, so I really prefer the looser kinds called *paniculata*, which have a flat central head fringed by open sterile flowers; a particularly pleasing variety is called *Sargentii*.

Among the brilliant climbers, *Bignonia grandiflora* with red-orange trumpets was as startling as the humble nasturtium in colour, but far more graceful and much taller in habit. It should never be planted against red brick, but against grey stone or against a white-washed cottage it looks both gay and splendid. (Nurserymen sometimes sell it under the name *Tecoma* or *Campsis radicans*.) The best variety is *Campsis Mme Galen*. Another orange climber, not quite so showy, goes by the unfortunate name of *Eccremocarpus scaber*; if I knew the English name for it, I would tell you. Perhaps it hasn't one. Not always considered quite hardy, it came through last winter unharmed. I notice also that that very lovely small flowering tree of white and gold, *Eucryphia intermedia*, has survived the winter; it is rather slow of growth, but all patient gardeners should plant at least one or two. It has the advantage of flowering while still quite young, in August just when such a stop-gap is most needed.

A reminder: bulbs for flowering in bowls next winter should now be planted in fibre, and kept in the dark till their little bleached noses show a couple of inches high. If a dark cupboard is not available, take the hint of a friend of mine who grew them most successfully under the sitting-room sofa.

August 7, 1949

It is not often that I mention vegetables, but I should like to put in a good word for the Globe artichoke. It appears to be almost unknown in this country. An enterprising greengrocer told me that he bought some in the market but had been obliged to throw them out, unsold, on to the rubbish heap. Yet there must surely be something to be said for a vegetable which is grown by the acre in such gastronomic countries as France and Italy.

There are three different kinds of artichoke: the Jerusalem, the Chinese, and the Globe. The Jerusalem, probably the best known in England, is a tuber and is a most insipid vegetable on which no epicure should waste time or space. (It has no connection with Jerusalem, by the way: the name is a corruption of *girasole*, turning-with-the-sun, the Italian for sunflower, to which the Jerusalem artichoke is botanically related.) The Chinese, also a tuber, is seldom met with but highly to be recommended. It is like a little whorled sea-shell to look at, and is very useful in winter when vegetables are scarce. Plant the tubers in rows in March; do not allow the plants to get too dry in summer; lift the tubers in November, and store in sand, using them as you require. Boil them first, and then fry them in a little butter.

But it is the Globe artichoke I really want to plead for. This is not a tuber, but a tall and extremely handsome plant with deeply indented grey-green leaves which are most decorative in the garden and splendid in a big vase of summer flowers; they have a sculptural, architectural quality, like the leaves of acanthus, which gives dignity to the gay, mixed bunch. It thus serves a double purpose, for even if you decide not to use it as a vegetable it can still be grown for its foliage and for the thistle-like purple heads which it will produce if allowed to flower. These, however, are the heads you ought to eat before they reach the flower-ing stage; and do eat them *young*, I beseech you, before they have had time to grow old and tough. There are many ways in which they can be cooked; you can either boil them, whole, in salted water for twenty to thirty minutes and then eat them hot or cold, with melted butter or oil and vinegar respectively; or divest them of their leaves, using only the bottom—what the French call *fonds d'artichaut*—in a variety of dishes, as an entrée with half a tomato sitting on top, or as a savoury with cheese sauce, or stuffed *à la Barigoule* . . . but this is not a cookery book, and any good recipe book will give you ideas. An old tradition, on which I was brought up, says that after eating an artichoke you should drink a glass of cold water to bring out the flavour.

The Globe artichoke admittedly takes up a good deal of room: at least three feet wide and six feet tall, it may seem out of proportion in a small kitchen garden, but, as I have suggested, it may be given a place in the flower garden for its decorative value alone. It likes full sun, and it should be planted in April. It is reasonably hardy, but to be on the safe side you might cover it with some litter, or bracken, or ashes, during the winter months or especially if you foresee late frosts in May when the young shoots are coming up. I have never bothered to do this, and my artichokes have come safely through some very hard winters, but I pass on the advice for what it is worth. The gardening books, also, will tell you to renew your plants every three years. They may be right. All I can say is that my own plants have been in my garden for over twelve years and show no sign of going off; they crop as well as ever and have received little attention, so on this point I must disagree with the gardening books. Practical experience is worth more than many pages of print.

For the comfort of northern readers, I find that an old book printed in 1832 records that 'Nowhere does the artichoke arrive at greater perfection than in the Orkney Islands.'

August 21, 1949

I wrote of flowering shrubs for July and August recently, but there were many that I had no space to mention. I omitted, for example, the Etna broom, *Genista aetnensis*, which always seems to astonish people and earns me a reputation that I do not at all deserve. It is no more difficult to obtain or to grow than any other broom; and if you plant it in the right place, by which I mean, in an angle against a dark background, it will display itself for several weeks in July rather like that firework known as Golden Rain, familiar to us all on village greens on the 5th of November. It is indeed a lovely thing, as light and frail as spume, pouring its mist of golden flowers from an eventual height of fifteen to twenty feet, so brilliant as to startle you when you come upon it round the corner. Do plant at least one; but insist on getting it *in a pot* from your nurseryman: it dislikes being dug up by its roots out of the ground.

I have planted hypericums under the Etna broom; they are young as yet, but will eventually flower at the same time, and I think their richer, heavier yellow will go well with the airy golden fountain overhead. These hypericums are the shrubby kind, not the ordinary low-growing St. John's Wort. They are *Hypericum patulum Henryii* and *Forrestii* for the most part, mixed with some treasured cuttings of better varieties, e.g. *H. Rowallane*, but if you just ask your nurseryman for the shrubby hypericum you cannot go far wrong. You will find that they will tolerate almost any ill-treatment; they will grow in shade or sun; they are most obliging, though on the whole they prefer a light soil; and for the housewife I may add that they are useful for cutting, every bud opening in water, day after day, which is a real consideration for one who has to 'do the flowers' in the house, and hasn't much time to renew fading blooms as they die.

The hydrangeas must be remembered for August; and there is *Buddleia alternifolia*, with long wands of purple, much more graceful than the common buddleia so attractive to all insects. *Clethra alnifolia*, the Sweet Pepperbush, has a tassel of white flowers with a good scent in August; not for northern gardeners but quite happy in the south.

Clerodendron Fargesii and *Clerodendron trichotomum* are stocky little trees not often seen in our gardens. Their flower is insignificant, but they are worth growing for the berries which succeed the flower. Turquoise-blue and scarlet, these clusters of berries look more like an artificial hat decoration. They are shiny, brilliantly coloured, and look as though they had been varnished. Try at least one sample in your garden. *Fargesii* is the better of the two.

August 6, 1950

This is not the first time I have written about herbs, and no doubt it will not be the last. My own small herb-garden is always encouragingly popular, with men as well as with the sentimentalists whom I know fatally in advance are going to say that it is full of old-world charm. Thus I make no apology for recording an excellent idea sent to me by an American correspondent. It is not arty-crafty, but severely practical, many herbs being great spreaders, whose invasion must be kept in check; and it seems to me just the thing for anybody who wants a herb-garden on a small scale, in a limited space.

You procure an old cart-wheel, the larger in diameter the better; you paint it white, with the outer rim green (where the iron tyre is), and sink the hub into a hole in the ground, so that the wheel will lie flush and level. This will give you a number of divisions in between the spokes in which to plant your herbs, plus the central hub, which you pierce through and fill with soil to grow one special, bushy little plant. (I suggest the dwarf dark purple lavender, Munstead variety.) My correspondent had fourteen divisions in which she planted chives, rue, sage, marjoram, basil, borage, balm, tansy, parsley, tarragon, rosemary, thyme, pennyroyal, and sage. Personally I should have included lovage, garlic, and caraway, but obviously the choice must be left to the grower.

She sent me a coloured photograph, and the effect of the flat white wheel, white spokes, and white hub was certainly very pretty, set in grass. Set in paving stones it might be even prettier. All round the edge of the wheel, between the spokes, she had painted the appropriate names of the herbs in red. Then she had had another bright idea: behind her wheel she had sunk a semicircle of large tins with the bottoms knocked out, and in these she grew the real spreaders, such as the mints, which were thus kept under control.

Of course one always tries to improve on other people's ideas, and I thought to myself that it would be better to grow nothing but low herbs between the spokes. Tall things, such as tansy, tarragon, and melilot, would quickly rise to destroy the flat, clock-face effect of the wheel. And then I thought how pretty it would be to grow not only herbs but small treasures of bulbs and Alpine plants in the same way, in pockets of specially made-up soil between the spokes: saxifrages, and Lewisias, and the tiny narcissi, and the specie irises, and *Anemone hepatica*, and all the miniature things that come out in the spring.

August 13, 1950

I revert to the subject of hedges, since they are so important in a garden, large or small; and, moreover, now that many people are moving into new houses with a plot of land demanding enclosure, the question of hedges becomes urgent: what to plant and when to plant it. Generally speaking, early autumn is the best time, and let us remember always that money spent on a good hedge is money well invested, for year by year it gives an increasingly good return.

Our American friends do not like hedges. They do not share our love of privacy, and maintain that if you plant a hedge round your garden you are doing something undemocratic and may even have 'something to hide.' Fortunately for us and for the beauty of our country we suffer from no such notions. We might well, however, display a little more imagination in our choice of hedging plants, instead of sticking with such depressing fidelity to privet, quick, *Lonicera nitida*, and *cupressus macrocarpa*.

There are two kinds of hedge, the useful and the ornamental. The useful hedge has the job of keeping animals out, and thus offers less scope for decorative informality, but life even in the country is not invariably a battle against cows or goats, and there are many plants

which will afford charm and colour as well as providing the
necessary line of demarcation. Rose hedges, for example,
promise to become increasingly popular, and what could
be lovelier than, say, a long stretch of some Hybrid Musk
or sweet-scented Rugosa? Again, I can imagine such evergreen flowering shrubs as *Osmanthus Delavayi* or *Choisya
ternata*, or the silver-leaved *Elæagnus macrophylla*, or the
many-coloured cydonias—incorrectly called japonicas—or
the many varieties of escallonia, especially valuable near the
sea. It would be impossible to give anything approaching a
complete list of suggestions here; but a most practical little
book has just come out, at the moderate price of 1s. 6d.:
Better Hedges, by Roy Hay, obtainable from Roy Hay
Publications, Dolphin Cottage, Grayswood, Haslemere.
Illustrated by photographs, it tells you how to plant; how
to cultivate; how to cut; how to renovate; and, most valuable
of all, ends up with eleven pages of special lists. These
include hedge plants for small gardens; plants for formal
or informal hedges; plants for the seaside, for semi-shade,
for light soils, for heavy soils, for chalky soils; and some
good hedge-plants for various situations and purposes, with
brief descriptions and instructions how to prune, trim and
clip. There is also a note on hedge-cutting with labour-
saving machinery.

August 20, 1950

At this time of the year, this dull time, this heavy August
time, when everything has lost its youth and is overgrown
and mature, the Japanese anemones come into flower with
a queer reminder of spring. They manage, in late summer,
to suggest the lightness of spring flowers. Tall, bold, stiff,
they come up every year, and may indeed be regarded as
a weed in the garden, so luxuriantly do they grow and
increase.

The common white anemone *Japonica alba* is the one

best known to us all. It is a most accommodating plant in many ways, because it does not resent being grown in half shade and is not particular as to soil. Neither does it require staking. It has a stiff resistant stalk. The only thing it resents is being moved. It takes at least two seasons to recover from removal; but when those two seasons have gone by, it will give you a rich return in white flowers with golden centres and a very long flowering period as bud after bud comes out. This alone makes it a satisfactory plant to grow in a shady or neglected corner where few other herbaceous plants would consent to flourish; but there are other varieties besides the common white, and it is to these that I would like to draw your attention.

The pale mauve one is, I suppose, almost as well known as the common white. It is very pretty, a lilac-mauve; but there are others, such as the variety called *Prince Henry*, a really deep mauve-pink, growing to a height of three to four feet and flowering from August to September. This will cost you 1s. 6d. a plant and is well worth it. There are also shorter ones, growing only to one or two feet, such as *Mont Rose*, which is described as old rose in colour, and *Profusion*, purplish-red, two feet high. I must confess that I have not grown *Mont Rose* or *Profusion* and know them only by repute; but *Prince Henry* grows in my garden, in a fortunate accidental association under the wine-coloured clematis *Kermesina*. This late-flowering clematis, belonging to the Viticella group of clematis, should be more often planted. It produces a mass of its small wine-coloured flowers, like a Burgundy wine held up to the light, at the very same time as the Japanese anemone *Prince Henry* comes to its best. They match one another to perfection.

My only grievance against the Japanese anemone is that it tires and droops once cut, and thus is no good for picking. But in the garden, however, it comes as a salvation in this dreary, uninteresting time of the year.

August 27, 1950

A lady asks me if she could make a miniature indoor garden on a large plate, 'if possible something bright for Christmas.' Well, it would have to be a very deep plate, almost a bowl, to give sufficient root-run if she wants her plants to be actually growing; and she would have to pierce holes at the bottom for drainage (which would not be easy, as the china would probably split in the process). This problem she could overcome by using the peat fibre supplied by sundriesmen for forcing bulbs in unpierced bowls, which for some mysterious reason does not require any outlet. I see no insuperable difficulty there. The only thing that worries me is the 'something bright for Christmas.'

There are few small bulbous plants which can be coaxed into flower by Christmas Day, at least not without a lot of forcing. There is the Paper-white narcissus, but this grows rather too tall for the sort of miniature garden my correspondent evidently has in mind; and there is the Roman hyacinth; but neither of these can accurately be described as bright. Some of the species crocuses might serve her purpose, and I have sent her an address (Messrs. Wallace, The Old Gardens, Tunbridge Wells), where she can procure these. But on the whole I think that for her Christmas plate she had better adopt another method, patiently leaving her miniature garden for a few weeks later. The Christmas-plate method I would suggest is to fill her plate with damp sand, covering it over with moss, and sticking into it any berried twig or coloured leaf or freakishly out-of-season flower such as a primrose or violet or a belated rose-bud or Christmas rose (hellebore). It is surprising what one can find, poking about, especially in a mild season, and a plateful of odds and ends can be extremely pretty and amusing.

After the New Year matters become much easier. If she plants up her plate in September with small bulbs, and keeps it in a dark cupboard until the growth is an inch or two high, then brings it out into the light (not too strong a light until the growth has turned quite green), she may expect a gay little picture in January or February. Whether she mixes her bulbs or keeps to one sort in each plate must depend on her personal taste. Scillas, grape-hyacinths, chionodoxa (Glory of the snow), crocus, iris reticulata, are all suitable for such treatment. A clump of snowdrops, lifted from the garden when its green noses begin to push through the soil, will come into flower in a surprisingly short time in a warm room. I have also dug up wild violets and primroses, and had them blooming very early.

I hope my correspondent will not introduce miniature gnomes or toadstools into her plate. She could, however, put a piece of looking-glass in the middle, not so much pretending to be a pool of water as to reflect and duplicate the heads of the little flowers growing around it.

September

September 29, 1946

THE two great planting months, October and November, are close upon us, and those gardeners who desire the maximum of reward with the minimum of labour would be well advised to concentrate upon the flowering shrubs and flowering trees. How deeply I regret that fifteen years ago, when I was forming my own garden, I did not plant these desirable objects in sufficient quantity. They would by now be large adults instead of the scrubby, spindly infants I contemplate with impatience as the seasons come round.

That error is one from which I would wish to save my fellow-gardeners, so, taking this opportunity, I implore them to secure trees and bushes from whatever nurseryman can supply them: they will give far less trouble than the orthodox herbaceous flower, they will demand no annual division, many of them will require no pruning; in fact, all that many of them will ask of you is to watch them grow yearly into a greater splendour, and what more could be exacted of any plant?

Your choice will naturally depend upon the extent of your garden, but it should be observed that any garden, however small, has a house in it, and that that house has walls. This is a very important fact to be remembered. Often I hear people say, 'How lucky you are to have these old walls; you can grow anything against them,' and then, when I point out that every house means at least four walls—north, south, east, and west—they say, 'I never thought of that.' Against the north and west sides you can grow magnolias or camellias; on the east side, which catches the morning sun, you can grow practically any of the hardy shrubs or climbers, from the beautiful ornamental quinces, commonly, though incorrectly, called Japonicas (the right name is Cydonia, or even more correctly, Chaemomeles, to the more robust varieties of *Ceanothus*, powdery-blue, or a blue fringing on purple. On the south side the choice is even larger—a vine, for instance, will soon cover a wide, high space, and in a reasonable summer will ripen its bunches of small, sweet grapes (I recommend Royal Muscadine, if you can get it); or, if you want a purely decorative effect, the fast-growing *Solanum crispum*, which is a potato though you might not think it, will reach to the eaves of the house and will flower in deep mauve for at least two months in early summer.

And apart from these wall-plants, many small trees may be set in convenient places. The flowering cherries and crabs have fortunately become a feature of most gardens, and how gaily they contribute to the aspect of English villages and cottages during the spring. Many of them, however, tend towards a rather crude pink; and those who would wish to avoid this colour may be better advised to plant the subtler greenish-white cherry called Ukon (*Cerasus Lannesiana grandiflora*) or the white-blossomed crab *Dartmouth*, with purplish-red fruits of remarkable beauty in the autumn; or that other crab, *Niedzwetzkyana*, with even more beautiful purple fruits. The almond, of course, will always be a favourite, partly because it flowers so early in the year; but if you are thinking of planting almonds now I would strongly recommend the variety called *Pollardii*, with a finer and deeper flower than the common kind usually seen.

The advantage of trees and shrubs is that they may be

underplanted with bulbs—another activity which should
not be neglected at this time of year. Daffodils, narcissi, and
hyacinths should be got into the ground without delay.
Bulbs are always a good investment, as they increase underground and may be lifted yearly, and the little offsets or
bulbils planted out in a spare corner to develop. Such raising
of one's own stock is much more satisfying than writing a
cheque or buying a postal order.

September 4, 1949

The autumn catalogues are beginning to arrive, and have
reminded me of the peonies. There are few more repaying
plants. Rabbits dislike them; their flowering season extends
through May and June; they last for a week or more as
picked flowers for the house; they will flourish in sun or
semi-shade; they will tolerate almost any kind of soil,
lime-free or otherwise; they will even put up with clay;
they never need dividing or transplanting; in fact, they
hate it; and they are so long-lived that once you have
established a clump (which is not difficult) they will probably
outlive you. Add to all this that they will endure neglect.
Mine struggled through the weeds of war and seem none
the worse for it.

Of course, if you want to do them well, they will respond
as any plant will respond to good treatment. If you have a
little bonemeal to spare, fork it in during the autumn. But
it is not really necessary. The only thing which is really
necessary is careful planting in the first instance, and by
this I mean that you should dig the hole eighteen inches
deep; put in some rotted manure or compost at the bottom;
fill it in with ordinary soil and *plant shallow*, i.e. don't bury
the crown more than a couple of inches underground.
This is important.

There are, roughly speaking, two different kinds of peony:
the herbaceous, in which we may include the species and

the Tree peony (*Paeonia suffruticosa*, or *Moutan*). The Tree peony is not very easy to get nowadays, and you would have to pay anything from 10s. 6d. to 30s. for it. Still, it is worth the investment, especially as it will start to flower young and will flower more and more copiously as it advances in age. *Never cut it down*. Mine were destroyed for ever by a jobbing gardener, who also happened (unbeknownst to me) to be a Jehovah's Witness, when he cut them to the ground one autumn.

The herbaceous peony is the one we are accustomed to see in some not very attractive shades of red or pink in cottage gardens. Do not condemn it on that account. There are now many varieties, either single or double, ranging from pure white through white-and-yellow to shell-pink, deep pink, and the sunset colour you find in *P. peregrina*. This really flames; and its companion, *P. lobata Sunbeam*, is as good, if not better. As a yellow I would recommend *P. Mlokosiewiczi*, did it not cost 30s. a plant; I grew it from a sixpenny packet of seed myself, but you have to be very patient to do that. Apart from this, *P. Laura Dessert* is probably the best yellow at the more reasonable price of 7s. 6d. *Sarah Bernhardt*, at 6s., has enormous pale pink flowers, double; *Kelway's Glorious*, at 12s. 6d., is a fine white; *Duchesse de Nemours*, at 5s., is white with a slightly yellowish tinge and smaller flowers; *Martin Cahuzac* at 6s., a dark red, has leaves which colour well in autumn.

Messrs. Kelway, Langport, Somerset, are large growers; and Mr. J. Russell, Sunningdale Nurseries, Windlesham, has a remarkable collection of the tree peonies.

September 18, 1949

This article is going to be concerned with two very different things: a tree and a lily. The tree, which is called *Koelreuteria apiculata*, is of astonishing beauty in August when it is fully grown to its eventual height of fifteen to

forty feet. For a tree to attain that height means waiting
for some years, and therefore this recommendation must be
addressed only to those who are responsible for the planting
of trees in any public park or garden or to those who intend
to stay put on their own plot of land: the owners of a freehold
country cottage, for instance. Vagrant tenants cannot afford
to wait so long.

I collected the seed of *Koelreuteria* in the abandoned
garden of an old abbey in France, having no idea what it
was. I could see only that it was of graceful growth, and was
dangling with seed-pods like little Chinese lanterns, or like
the pods of that plant we call the Cape gooseberry (*Physalis
capensis*), and grow for winter decoration. Sown in a pan
when I got them home, my seeds sprouted as generously
as grass; I soon had a potential forest. I planted some
seedlings out, and I did notice that the leaves turned
a very pretty pink colour, but it was not until I saw a full-
grown specimen in a neighbour's garden that I realized
what a treasure I had got hold of. This specimen was in full
flower; bright yellow flowers borne on erect spikes about a
foot tall, something like Golden Rod if you can imagine
Golden Rod growing out of a tree right above your head,
standing up boldly above tasselled masses of coral-pink
seed-pods, and the leaves of a light feathery green. I do not
exaggerate. The effect, against the blue sky, was amazing.

The lily I want to write about is *L. regale*, that sweet-
scented trumpet which is perhaps the easiest of that tricky
family to grow. There is no connection between it and the
Koelreuteria except that they both come so easily from seed.
Now the current price for flowering bulbs ranges from 16s.
to 20s. a dozen, so if you want them in any quantity it will
pay you to raise them from seed, and this is the moment to
look out for seeding heads in your own or a friend's garden.
You can also buy seed for 6d. to 1s. a packet, but it is more
fun to crack open a seed-pod and shake out those mar-

vellously packed, paper-thin seeds for yourself. Every one
of them should germinate, and one pod alone should give
you more lilies than you will ever have space for. Choose
the seeds from the strongest plant; sow them in a seed box
and plant out the little bulbs next year in rows in a nursery
bed where you can keep an eye on them; by the end of the
second year you ought to be picking a few single flowers;
by the end of the third year they ought to be fully developed.
If you repeat the process yearly, thus staggering your
supply of bulbs, you should never be without *L. regale* in
your garden, at no cost.

You realize, of course, that you can do the same with
those little black boot-buttons that appear on the stems of
the old tiger-lily?

I cannot resist adding a note at a later date (1950) to
pass on an amusing hint for growing lilies from seed. You
need a screw-top jar, such as housewives bottle fruit in; a
mixture of leaf-mould, peat, and loam, enough to fill the
jar; and half a handful of seed. You make the mixture wet,
and then squeeze it in your hand till it stops dripping and
becomes a damp sponge. You then introduce it into the jar,
sowing the seed in layers as you go, until the mixture and
the seed have both reached the rim. You then screw on the
top; put the jar on the window-sill in a warm room, and
watch for the seeds which have come to the edge, where
you can see them, to develop into little tadpole-like bodies
which, you hope, will eventually become bulbs.

September 3, 1950

Reproachful letters reach me: how *can* I say that the
August garden is dull and heavy? These letters are all
courteous and kindly, but it is evident that their writers are
pained. Several of them paint a picture of such gaiety that
I remain abashed. It is, of course, perfectly true that if you
have time for the annuals (and not too large a space to fill)

you can have a blaze of colour lasting well into September. It was not difficult to visualize the swagger patches that my correspondents were looking at: petunias, ageratum, snapdragons, portulaca, cosmea, arctotis, larkspur, stocks, verbena, zinnias . . . the very thought of them made me blink. And to these must be added such perennials as the heleniums, the flat-headed yellow achillea, the rudbeckias, the gaillardias (there are two particularly fine ones, called *Tangerine* and *Wirral Flame*). And dahlias. And gladioli. And montbretia. Yes, perhaps I was wrong. I was probably thinking more of the sluggish trees, the overgrown hedges, the brambles bringing their first hint of autumn; and thus must acknowledge that my aversion to the August garden may be psychological rather than factual. I just cannot bear feeling that summer is petering out to its end, and spring so far behind.

As I have indicated, I don't grow many annuals except the zinnias, to which I am always faithful. There is, however, one which proved very decorative this year and remained in flower for a very long time; in fact, it is flowering still. This was *Venidium fastuosum*, a half-hardy South African daisy of enormous size, three inches wide at least, of the most brilliant, varnished-looking orange petals and a central ring of darkness round the base. Why, I wondered, looking into the heart of this garish thing, should Nature take so much trouble and display such inventiveness? Why such superfluous ingenuity? Why this eternal, inexplicable miracle of variation? Was it intended to appeal to us as human beings or to some insect in search of nectar?

There are hybrids of *Venidium* which should be worth trying, though *V. fastuosum* is probably the best. The hybrids are described in catalogues as ranging in colour from white to lemon and straw; there is also a dwarf strain, about a foot high, in yellow and orange. If one has facilities for starting them early, in boxes under glass, as is the usual practice with half-hardy annuals, they would, of course, come earlier into flower; but otherwise a sowing made out of doors towards the end of May, where they are intended to remain, would start flowering at the beginning of July and should continue right through August.

September 10, 1950

I wrote once in this column about a little lawn I had made of the cultivated or garden sorts of the common creeping thyme, but this article is going to be about the other sorts, too bushy or too wiry to be suitable for such a purpose. A narrow bed in a sunny place, say under a shed or a house wall, filled with a collection of various thymes, could be very charming and sweet-scented, and a great pleasure to the bees. It has the advantage of preferring a poor, stony soil, such as you often find against a construction where the builders have left their rubbish of rubble, mortar, and grit; places where greedier plants will refuse to grow without the enormous trouble of first redeeming the waste.

This consideration will doubtless appeal to the practical gardener quite as much as the more romantic associations with thyme. We have perhaps now forgotten that 'to smell of thyme' was a phrase used by the Greeks to express a literary elegance of style; or that medieval ladies embroidered a sprig of thyme surmounted by a bee, to denote courage as supplied by a decoction of thyme, and activity as demonstrated by the insect; or that an elaborate preparation of thyme enabled you to see fairies; or that it was 'very good to be given in either phrenzy or lethargy'; or that it cured you of the nightmare, and also of the melancholy.

There are said to be twenty-four different kinds of thyme, but few people will aspire to a complete assemblage.

In a narrow bed such as I have imagined, say a couple of feet wide, I should be satisfied with half-a-dozen varieties. In the front I should plant low-growing kinds: *thymus lanuginosus*, the grey woolly thyme, and *thymus herba-barona*, which is also known as the Caraway thyme because of its peculiar scent, but which gets its official name because it was used to flavour that massive lump, the Baron of Beef.

Behind these low-growers I should plant the shrubby kinds. The golden thyme, *T. citriodorus aureus*, and the silvery thyme, *T. citriodorus argenteus*, both lemon-scented, as their name implies; and *T. ericafolius*, which is a heather-like shrublet, green tinged with yellow; and *T. nitidus*, about a foot high, with purple flowers.

It is possible to buy plants of all these, and seed of some of them, to be sown in March or early April; though it is said that the lemon-scented kinds will smell sweeter if raised from cuttings or little rooted bits, taken any time from May to September. It is thus not too late to beg for scraps, or to order from a nurseryman (a list of addresses is given on p. 237), for planting out this autumn. May I also suggest that a planting of small spring-flowering bulbs amongst them would give interest and colour in the early months of the year?

September 17, 1950

For two or three years past I have been trying to run to earth a plant called *Tropaeolum polyphyllum*, a native of Chile. 'Run to earth' is indeed the right phrase, for it buries itself so deep in the ground that it is impossible to dig up. All efforts to obtain a tuber from the garden of a friend, where it grows like a weed, proved vain; it simply snapped off, and for all I know the essential tuber was half way down between Kent and the Antipodes. Now, however, in one week, I have found it advertised by two separate nurserymen, one of whom remarks that 'for some reason it has become rather rare.'

It should not be allowed to become rare, for it is a very showy, decorative thing, flowering in June, in long creeping trails of bright yellow nasturtium-like trumpets extending nearly a yard long from its grey-green leaves. I cannot improve upon the description given by one of the nursery-men listing it: 'It makes a wonderful effect with its glaucous foliage and garlands of blossom.' It certainly does. It looks like golden serpents writhing out of a sea-green base. The ideal place to plant it, I imagine, would be in a dry wall, say in some Cotswold garden, when it could tuck its roots into cool crevices and could allow its garlands of blossom to pour in golden waterfalls down some small vertical cliff of that lovely stone. Alternately it would look well in a rock garden, for it seems to demand stone to set it off, and thus is not so suitable for a bed or border.

The moral of its preference for deep rooting is to plant it deep at the outset, at least a foot to eighteen inches. I imagine that like its relation *Tropaeolum speciosum*, the flame-coloured nasturtium which does so brilliantly in Scotland and so poorly in England, it would not object to partial shade. Do not be alarmed when it disappears entirely during the winter: it will reappear in spring. It also has the pleasant habit of rambling about through anything which may be planted near it, and of coming up in unex-pected places. *

A useful clematis flowering in September is *Clematis flammula*. I would not advocate it for an important or prominent place, as its masses of small white flowers are not in the least showy, but for scrambling over a rough shed or outhouse, where its peculiarly musty scent may be caught by the passer-by. Its great virtue is that it will flourish in

* Messrs. Pennell, Lincoln, and Mr. Cusack, whose address is on p. 119, both list it.

places which never get any sun, the picture of contentment
on a cruelly dark north wall. There is a pale pink variety,
which might be more pleasing, but I cannot speak from
experience.

September 24, 1950

Catalogues arrive by every post, and are as bewildering in
their diversity as in their monotony. What shall we order
this autumn? Bulbs, shrubs, flowering trees, herbaceous
plants, or what? How tempting the lists are! And how easy
they make gardening sound! If you believed half they say
you would look forward next year to a garden something
between Kew and the tropical estate of some legendary
millionaire in Guatemala. It is difficult to keep one's head.
I always lose mine. Year after year I am decoyed into experiments which I know are almost certainly doomed to
failure. I cannot resist. Experience tells me that I ought to
resist, but, like the poor mutt who falls to the card-sharper
in the train, I fall to every list offering plants I cannot afford
to buy and could not cultivate successfully even if I could
afford them.

I have, however, received from Ireland a catalogue of
such enchantment that it makes me revoke all my cautious
mean resolutions. This Irish nurseryman is a man after my
own heart. He writes of his wares in a lively, unstereotyped
style, starting off grandly with 'I like them all, or I would
not have them in my list.' He is meticulous as to colour:
'I call mauve mauve,' he says, 'not blue.' He likes species,
'as nature made them, unhybridized by man, undistorted
by his whim.' Then I like his vigour. Writing of *Eremurus
robustus* he says: 'Robust it is, by Jove!—with lovely strong
pink spires rocketing up to ten feet,' and describes the roots
of *eremurus* as apocryphal spiders. And he ends up with a
plea that only a very disillusioned heart could disregard,
'Please do try some of those plants you may never have

heard of '—which, after all, is the philosophy I myself have been preaching ever since I took to writing these articles.

Admittedly, many of his plants are for the connoisseur, but we can all find a special corner for treasures, and on the whole his claims for the ease with which they may be grown are not too madly exaggerated. I cannot go all the way with him over the blue Chilean, *Tecophilea cyanocrocus*, for instance, that incredibly lovely thing which, as he rightly remarks, must be seen to be believed; or over *Ixia viridiflora*, which I have always found less reliable than the other ixias. Where I find myself in complete agreement is over his insistence on good drainage, for I am convinced that the enemy in these islands is damp rather than frost, and this, I suppose, must be his worry in Ireland even more than it is ours in England. I might add that his prices are low, even in comparison with those of some Dutch bulb-growers.

His address is: Ralph Cusack, Uplands, Roundwood, Co. Wicklow.

October

October 27, 1946

STRAWBERRIES at the end of October, at negligible expense and negligible trouble. This does not mean that they will fruit *only* by October; it means that having fruited generously throughout the summer, from June onwards, they will continue to carry their crop until the first frost; I have, in fact, picked them so late as November.

This exemplary plant is the Alpine strawberry. The new garden varieties carry a much larger berry than the *fraises des bois*, which provide so frequent and delicious a feature of meals in Continental restaurants, and they certainly equal them in flavour. To enumerate their virtues deserves a whole paragraph. First, they require no straw, since the fruit is well up among the leaves, and only a berry here and there will rest upon the ground to become a prey for slugs. Then, for some extraordinary reason, the birds take no interest in them; consequently, no netting is necessary. Then, if a late frost should spoil the blossom, new blossom soon appears, which is more than can be said for the ordinary strawberry. Finally, they are neat little plants, and make a charming edging along a path, taking up very little room and being indeed quite decorative with their bright red berries and soft green leaves.

The best variety to grow as an edging is the runnerless *Baron Solemacher*; the sort called *Cresta*, which makes many runners, is rather untidy and is better in a bed to itself. There is also a runnerless *Strawberry Delight*, which can be had with a pale yellow as well as a red berry, but of this I cannot speak from personal acquaintance.

Their demands? Farmyard manure or compost will of course increase their luxuriance, but I have found them doing quite well without it in a reasonably good soil. They seem to prefer a little shade, where they become jucier and more luscious; and they must be picked very ripe, over-ripe if anything. One important point concerns the actual eating: they should be picked two or three hours in advance, then pricked with a fork or even slightly crushed, powdered with sugar, and left to stand in a bowl. If you can add a spoonful of red wine, or sherry or Madeira, so much the better; but perhaps that is a counsel of perfection.

To this hint for epicures, I should like to add a plea for greater enterprise in next year's kitchen garden. A grey monotony attends our English vegetables . . . and not only in their cooking. *Calabrese* as a change from cabbage; *Hamburg Parsley* instead of parsnips, or grated raw into a salad; *celeriac*, so useful in winter; Chinese artichokes instead of Jerusalem; the Globe artichoke, too, seldom seen in English gardens, though it is ornamental as well as useful; sorrel, which may be used like spinach, or to make soup. Potatoes, too, need not always be huge, floury, and somewhat insipid; try *Belle de Juillet*, or *Rosa* or *Kipfler*, if you can get them. Messrs. Harrison, Maidstone, usually have them.

Herbs would require an article to themselves. I suppose that every cook has by now discovered the virtues of chives, but how many insist upon a plant of lovage, which, with shredded leaves, makes all the difference to sandwiches and salads? And how many gardeners bother to grow caraway, which is as easy as mustard-and-cress, sows itself everywhere, and yet produces plenty of seed?

Dill, associated in most people's minds with dill-water for

babies, is almost indistinguishable from caraway in taste, and, moreover, is very pretty in a mixed bunch of summer flowers, with its flat greenish-yellow heads and upright carriage.

All very well if you live in the country, with a herb-garden just outside the kitchen door, not necessarily larger than the top of the kitchen table, but what about the town dwellers? For their consolation, it is surprising how many herbs will flourish in a window-box, Chives not the most despicable amongst them.

October 12, 1947

A new pleasure has abruptly entered my life, and I should like to pass it on to others: the Strawberry grape. It is per-fectly hardy here in Kent, where an outdoor specimen, twenty years old, covers a cottage, and is now heavy with ruby-pink bunches this autumn even after the cruel winter of 1946–47. My own little vine is only in its second year, but is already fruiting so generously that a number of bunches had to be suppressed; it would have been unwise as well as unkind to let so young a thing carry more than eight. But I foresee that it will go on in strength and wealth.

The great point about this grape is its flavour. I hope the professional nurseryman will forgive me if I say that his claims for his wares sometimes read better on paper than they turn out in fact; his colours blow brighter, his fruit tastes sweeter, and the vigour of his plants is beyond belief. But the Strawberry grape really does taste of strawberries—the little Alpine or wood strawberry. One unkind guest said it tasted of peardrops, but I stick to my conviction.

A single plant will cost you 10s. 6d., but will, I am sure, prove an investment paying a good dividend. It can be ob-tained from The Six Hills Nursery, Stevenage, Hertfordshire.

Another vine which is giving me great pleasure at the moment is *Vitis heterophylla*, an East Asian. You can't eat it, but you can pick it and put it in a little glass on your table, where its curiously coloured berries and deeply cut leaves look oddly artificial, more like a spray designed by a jeweller out of dying turquoises than like a living thing. Yet it will grow as a living thing, very rapidly, on the walls of your house, or over a porch, hanging in lovely swags of its little blue berries, rather subtle, and probably not the thing that your next-door-neighbour will bother to grow or perhaps doesn't know about. There are some obvious plants which we all grow: useful things, and crude. We all know about them. But the real gardener arrives at the point when he wants something rather out of the common run; and that is why I make these suggestions which might turn your garden into something a little different and a little more interesting than the garden of the man next door.

A note on some special small trees for autumn colour may therefore not come amiss. *Cratægus Crus-Galli*, the Cockspur Thorn, turns as scarlet as you could wish in October, and is a tough little tree which will flourish anywhere; against the dark background of a hedge he will look splendid. *Disanthus cercidifolius* hangs itself with round leaves like golden coins. *Cornus Kousa* and *Cornus florida rubra*; *Berberis Thunbergii atropurpurea splendens*; *Parrotia persica*; *Prunus Sargentii*; all these will flame throughout October until the leaves come off. It is a good plan to plant them where at some moment of the day they will catch the sunlight; and it is more effective to plant two or three in a clump than some isolated specimen. This advice applies to most plants, but especially to those designed to make a bonfire of colour in the rich, mellow days of autumn.

October 2, 1949

The blue trumpets of *Gentiana sino-ornata* have given great pleasure during September. Some people seem to think they are difficult to grow, but, given the proper treatment, this is not true. They like semi-shade (I grow mine round the foot of an apple tree, which apparently suffices them in this respect); they like plenty of moisture, which does mean that you have to water them every other evening in an exceptionally dry summer; and they utterly abhor lime. This means that if you have a chalky soil you had better give up the idea of growing these gentians unless you are prepared to dig out a large, deep hole and fill it entirely with peat and leaf-mould.

It is a safe rule that those plants which flourish in a spongy mixture of peat and leaf-mould will not tolerate lime; and the gentians certainly revel in that sort of mixture. As a matter of fact, I planted mine in pure leaf-mould and sand without any peat, and they seem very happy. Perhaps they would have been even happier with some handfuls of Sorbex peat thrown in. But I am quite satisfied, and so are they. The boxful of plants I set out last autumn, the gift of a kind friend in Scotland who says she has to pull them up like weeds in her garden (lucky woman), have now grown into so dense a patch that I shall be able to treble it next year.* For the gentian has the obliging habit of layering itself without any assistance from its owner, and I have now discovered that every strand a couple of inches long has developed a system of sturdy white roots, so that I can detach dozens of little new plants in March without disturbing the parent crown, and, in course of time, can carpet yards of ground with gentian if I wish, and if my supply of leisure, energy, and leaf-mould will run to it.

Gentiana sino-ornata is very low-growing, four inches high at most, but although humble in stature it makes up for its dwarfishness by its brilliance of colour, like the very best bit of blue sky landing by parachute on earth. By one of those happy accidents which sometimes occur in gardening,

* I have.

I planted my gentians near a group of the tiny pink autumn cyclamen, *Cyclamen europaeum*, which flowers at exactly the same time. They look so pretty together, the blue trumpets of the gentian and the frail, frightened, rosy, ears-laid-back petals of the cyclamen: they share something of the same small, delicate quality. It is one of the happiest associations of flowers.

So please plant *Gentiana sino-ornata* in a leaf-mould shady bed in your garden, with an inter-planting of *Cyclamen europaeum*. The same conditions will suit them both. The gentian may cost you anything up to 16s. 6d. a dozen; but even half a dozen will give you as many plants as you need in a year's time; and as for the cyclamen, its brown bun of a corm seems immortal, with a rich progeny of seedlings coming up all over the place.

October 16, 1949

Some friends of mine planted a small peach tree six years ago. They stuck it in and left it to make what it could of itself. This year they have picked over 900 peaches from it, fine large fruits, excellent for dessert, for jam or for bottling. We usually associate peaches with a sunny wall— and how warm the rosy fruit looks, hanging against old brick of much the same colour—but this tree stands out in the open, unsheltered, unprotected, and unpruned. The branches had to be propped, they were so heavy; but apart from a generous mulch of manure, that was all the attention it got. A good reward, I thought, for so little trouble.

Of course, if you could find a sheltered corner, say in the angle formed by two hedges, giving protection from cold winds, it might do even better; and there is no doubt that if you threw a veil of tiffany or butter-muslin or even some old lace curtains over the blossom when frost threatens in April or May, you would be doing much to safeguard the crop. This would apply especially in a hard winter and a draughty spring. My friends treated their tree rough: they let it take its chance, and it took it. So I thought I would advise other people to try the same experiment.

After all, what do you risk? A guinea to buy the tree. Then you wait for a year or two, and then you start to pick the fruit. You get a couple of dozen after three years. After six years you get 900—not a bad investment. It would certainly succeed in the Home Counties and in the South, and I have heard of a regular orchard of peaches in Essex, though I should not like to venture an opinion about the North. But, given a reasonably mild district, there seems no reason why this experiment should not be turned into profit as well as pleasure. The importation of foreign fruit has not improved the English market, but the home grower can still sell peaches or nectarines for anything up to eightpence each, and 900 eightpences would make a useful contribution to the current expenses involved in keeping up a garden.

The peach my friends grow is called *Grosse Mignonne*, and that has proved its quality; but varieties specially recommended for this rather unorthodox method, i.e. not fan-trained against a wall, are *Peregrine*, *Sea Eagle*, and *Duke of York*.

I have mentioned nectarines. This most delicious fruit could, of course, be grown in the same way, as a bush in the open. *Early Rivers* and *Humboldt* are both good varieties.

October 30, 1949

It always surprises me that we in this country should neglect to plant some of the fruits which are now seldom to be seen save as survivals in some old garden. For example, the common quince. In some parts of France you see it growing as a hedgerow plant, its great yellow pear-shaped fruits heavily hanging for any thrifty villager to pick and turn into jelly or quince-cheese. It grows in the hedgerows there as thick as blackberries in an English lane. Why don't we plant it in our gardens here, as our grandfathers did?

It is of the easiest possible cultivation, and will do in almost any type of soil, though naturally it will be happiest in a nice light loam with plenty of humus. It appreciates moisture, so long as it is not completely waterlogged. It requires no pruning or spraying. So far as I know, it suffers from no form of disease.* It is self-fertile. Birds do not attack it, and the fruit ripens too late for the wasps. The blossom comes late, and thus seldom has to endure danger from frost. It lives to a great age and is a regular and reliable cropper. It makes all the difference to stewed apples or to an apple-pie. It can, and should, be turned as I have said into delicious jelly, marmalade, or cheese. If it is on its own roots, as it usually is, it can be readily increased from its own suckers. To this catalogue of excellences, add that it is very beautiful, both in May when it flowers and in October when it ripens, and you will not wonder that I should demand a revival of planting the common quince.

So far as its beauty goes, I think there are two ideal situations to choose for it. One would be near water, so that the branches would hang over and be reflected in a pool, a stream, or even a pond. The other would be immediately beneath a bedroom window, so that in the spring you could look down into the wide upturned faces of the shell-pink blossom amongst the young leaves and the wiry tangle of very black twigs, and in the autumn on to the fat golden fruits. Only the occupant of that upper room could tell the delight of observing the quince throughout the cycle of the seasons.

Then, as a postscript, I might put in a good word for the bullace. This, like the quince, is a tree seldom seen except in old gardens. It is, I believe, the child of a marriage

* Note: see page 140.

between a damson and a plum. It has no ornamental value, but crops inordinately every year, small purple fruits which bring a good marketing price if you have the patience and leisure to pick them, and can also be used to make bullace wine.

As for the cherry-plum, or *myrobalan*, the medlar, and the various gages, including the old greengage, I must leave those for another article.*

October 1, 1950

I know I am continuously grousing about the dearth of plants, apart from annuals and herbaceous stuff, to enliven the garden in August and September, so it was with a startled pleasure that I observed three bushes growing in a cottage garden as I drove along a secret lane. They looked like pink lilac. Tall, pyramidal in shape, smothered in pointed panicles of flower, they suggested a bush of pink lilac in May. Yet this was September. . . . Puzzled, I stopped by the roadside to investigate.

It was *Hydrangea paniculata grandiflora*, sometimes called the plumed hydrangea. In its native country, Japan, it is said to attain a height of twenty-five feet, but in this country it apparently limits itself to something between six and eight feet; and quite enough, too, for the average garden. Do not confuse it with *H. hortensis*, the one which sometimes comes sky-blue but more often a dirty pink, and which is the one usually seen banked up in Edwardian opulence against the grandstand of our more fashionable race-courses. *H. paniculata grandiflora*, in spite of its resounding name, is less offensively sumptuous and has a far subtler personality.

It reveals, for instance, a sense of humour, and even of fantasy in the colouring it adopts throughout its various stages. It starts off by flowering white; then turns into the pink I have already described as looking like pink lilac.

* Addresses of fruit-growers will be found on p. 236.

Then it turns greenish, a sort of sea-green, so you never know where you are with it, as you never know where you are with some human personalities, but that makes them all the more interesting. Candidly white one moment; prettily pink the next; and virulently green in the last resort. . . . As I was leaning over the gate, looking at this last pink-green inflorescence, the tenant of the cottage observed me and came up. Yes, he said, it has been in flower for the last three months. It changes its colour as the months go by, he said. He knew it was a hydrangea, though he couldn't remember its second name. He was very proud of it. He was a dark man, a foreigner: and although he spoke fluent English he had a thick, peculiar accent which I could not identify. As I was talking to him across his gate, a circus passed with all its caravans and roundabouts; and I thought that the foreign man, and the circus, and the English cottage garden were all very much of the same thing; and that I would certainly order *H. paniculata grandiflora* to grow in a damp, shady spot next year, and hoped it would do as well as his.

October 8, 1950

My apologies for the delay in sending the Irish nurseryman's address. I have only just returned from abroad to find many letters of inquiry. I am now only hoping that he may be able to cope with the orders he receives, and that no one may be disappointed.

It was too late in the year to find many wild flowers in the mountains or in Italy, though in France the meadows were mauve with the autumn crocus and in the Apennines the woods and banks were stippled a shy pink with the little cyclamens. It was tantalizing to pass hill-slopes green with what appeared to be turf, but which on investigation proved to be a solid mat of *Gentiana acaulis*. I arrived in Tuscany with a bag full of seed and bulbs, corms and tubers; goodness knows whether they will consent to flower next year in

England or what some of them will turn out to be; but at least one shining flower reminded me of itself, with a kind of reproach for not being more common in our gardens. This was *Sternbergia lutea*, the lily-of-the-field. They toiled not, neither did they spin, but they were certainly arrayed in beauty as they spread themselves in a gilded carpet under the black cypresses framing a distant view of Florence.

Sternbergia lutea might easily be mistaken for a crocus. It is, in fact, neither a crocus nor a lily, despite its scriptural association; it belongs to the family of the amaryllis. It is a most brilliant yellow, varnished as a buttercup, rising crocus-like amongst its narrow leaves. It likes a rather rich, gravelly soil, well drained, with as much sun-baking as possible. It does not like being disturbed; it likes being left for years in a clump to develop, with a little protection of bracken or leaf-litter through the winter in this country. It costs about 1s. 3d. a bulb, or 12s. a dozen, from English nurserymen. It is a very old plant in English gardens, having been mentioned by John Parkinson in the reign of Charles the First; Parkinson called it the Great Autumn Daffodil, though of course it is no more a daffodil than it is a crocus or a lily. I shall think of it always as I saw it growing in its golden sprinkle on that Florentine terrace, beneath the cypresses framing the cupola of the Duomo and the tower of the Palazzo Vecchio, romantic, floodlit; the lily tower of Florence.

*   *   *

May I remind readers that the W.V.S. makes a special autumn appeal for plants, herbaceous or otherwise, which gardeners may now be discarding? It is better, surely, that they should go to beautify some stark pre-fab. or bare housing estate, than perish on the bonfire? Your local W.V.S. will collect them, with no expense to yourself, if you will kindly advise them.

October 15, 1950

The autumn garden. . . . It has its beauty; especially, perhaps, a garden with an old orchard attached to it. When I was very small, about four years old, I suppose, a line of poetry entered into my consciousness, never to leave it again:

Rye pappels drop about my head.

I had no idea what rye pappels might be, but they held a magic, an enchantment for me, and when in later life I identified them as the ripe apples of Andrew Marvell's poem they had lost nothing of their enchantment in the process of growing up.

Coming home from abroad, after an interval when the season had time to change from late summer into autumn, it struck me how *pink* and green the autumn garden was. Not bronze and blue, the colours we associate with the turning woods and the hazy distance and the blue smoke of bonfires along the hedgerows. The woods had not turned yet, but in the orchard the apples were rosy and in the garden the leaves of the peonies were pink, and so were the leaves of the common azaleas, and so were the leaves of *Parrotia persica* and the leaves of that other little tree with the lovely name *Liquidamber*, and the leaves of *Prunus Sargentii*, so soon to drop, alas, from the row in which I had planted them along the top of a rosy-red brick retaining-wall.

The naked, reddish stems of the Belladonna lily (*Amaryllis*) had shot up in that surprising way they have, and were opening their clusters of pink flowers. This is a bulbous plant well worth growing, for it is reasonably hardy in the open ground in a sunny, well-drained position, preferably at the foot of a wall, and it supplies flowers for picking at a time when choice-looking flowers are rare. What it likes is lots of water in the early summer, while it is making its leaves, and then it likes to be left alone while the leaves disappear and nothing is seen until the flowering stems shoot up all of a sudden on an October morning. It may seem a bit expensive to buy (1s. 9d. to 2s. 6d. a bulb); but once you have got it you have got it for keeps, which is more than can be said for a two-and-sixpenny seat at a cinema.

The Michaelmas daisies were also rioting pink in the garden. All the sorts called *Beechwood, Beechwood Charm, Beechwood Challenger*, and that specially good one called *Harrington's Pink*. Some people tell me that *Harrington's Pink* is not a good doer. I can say only that it does very well here in ordinary conditions, and that I have no complaint to make against it. It thrives, adding its bit of brighter pink to the rich scale of colouring leaves in the incarnadine symphony of October.

October 22, 1950

In my garden I have an awkward little border. It is awkward only in the sense that I have never made up my mind how best to use it. I have tried many things, and nothing has ever looked right, except the wine-coloured and ruby-coloured wallflowers in the spring. These have to be torn out towards the middle of May, when they are over and the little border is then left blank and empty, piteously clamouring for something to restore life to it during the summer. My little border, about a yard wide, happens to run along the foot of an old wall, this garden being largely a walled garden; but there are many narrow borders running under the house-wall, warm and sheltered, where one would wish to make the gayest possible display from April up to the autumn. The wallflowers are *right*; but what comes later? I have tried Korean chrysanthemums; no, they were too tall. I have tried annual carnations; no, they were too floppy. So now I have had another idea.

It was suggested to me by coming again across that pretty word: mixty-maxty. The dictionary defines it as 'incongruously or promiscuously mingled; jumbled together;

mixed; confused.' Very well, I thought, a mixty-maxty border it shall be. I will buy many packets of annuals, and sow them on the ground as soon as the wallflowers have been thrown away; but I shall not sow them according to the usual method, a patch of larkspur at the back, a patch of candytuft at the front, all regulated by their different heights and colours; I shall tear open all my packets and pour all the seeds out into an old tobacco tin, and shake them up together, and then sow them and let them take their chance. Very odd effects may result. I may get a tall spire coming up in front, and a dwarf hidden at the back, but I shall not care. The fun of gardening is nothing unless you take reckless risks.

All the same, despite recklessness, one must also be sensible. Let us now come down to brass tacks. One must draw up a list of annuals for sowing. One might include some half-hardy annuals, since they will not be sown until the latter half of May. Here is a rough draft of my list, my half-sensible, half-temerarious list, of the seeds I propose to order and shake up in a tin and scatter broadcast along that narrow border. They are all seeds which can be obtained at a very low price from any of the big seedsmen.

Phacelia campanularia. Cornflower. Salpiglossis. Zinnias. Cosmea. Coreopsis. Clarkia. Eschscholtzia. Love-in-a-mist. Petunias. Godetia. Salvia patens. Scabious. Larkspur. Verbenas. *

October 29, 1950

October is the time for the garden to be taken to pieces and replanted if necessary for next year. It is also the month that ushers in the long dark evenings when one makes seed lists under the lamp, pure pleasure and no worry; no slugs, no rabbits, no moles, no frosts, no damping-off. An interesting and unusual plant which should find a place is

* July 1951. Do not follow this advice. It was a complete failure.

Cobaea scandens, which sounds more attractive under its English name of cups-and-saucers. This is a climber, and an exceedingly rapid one, for it will scramble eight to ten feet high in the course of a single summer. Unfortunately it must be regarded as an annual in most parts of this country, and a half-hardy annual at that, for although it might be possible with some protection to coax it through a mild winter, it is far better to renew it every year from seed sown under glass in February or March. Pricked off into small pots in the same way as you would do for tomatoes, it can then be gradually hardened off and planted out towards the end of May. In the very mild counties it would probably survive as a perennial.

It likes a rich, light soil, plenty of water while it is growing, and a sunny aspect. The ideal place for it is a trellis nailed against a wall, or a position at the foot of a hedge, when people will be much puzzled as to what kind of a hedge this can be, bearing such curious short-stemmed flowers, like a Canterbury Bell with tendrils. Unlike the Canterbury Bell, however, the flowers amuse themselves by changing their colour. They start coming out as a creamy white; then they turn apple-green, then they develop a slight mauve blush, and end up a deep purple. A bowl of the mixture, in its three stages, is a pretty sight, and may be picked right up to the end of October. *

If you are now thinking that a half-hardy annual such as *Cobaea scandens* is too much trouble, and perhaps want something more permanent than you can get out of a seed packet, do consider the rose called *Nevada*. It got an Award of Merit from the R.H.S. in 1949, and well it deserved it. I do not think I have mentioned it before, and as it is a fairly new rose, you may not have come across it. This is not a climber, but a shrubby type, forming an arching bush

* The seed is obtainable from Messrs. Thompson & Morgan, Ipswich, Suffolk, or from Mr. Thomas Butcher, Shirley, Croydon, Surrey.

up to seven or eight feet in height, smothered with great single white flowers with a centre of golden stamens. One of its parents was the Chinese species rose *Moyesii*, which created a sensation when it first appeared and has now become well known. For those who are interested in such pedigrees, the other parent was *La Giralda*, a cross between that grand old Hybrid Perpetual, *Frau Karl Druschki*, and *Mme Edouard Herriot*. The grievance against *Moyesii* is that it flowers only once, in June; but *Nevada*, unlike *Moyesii*, has the advantage of flowering at least twice during the summer, in June and again in August, with an extra trickle of odd flowers right into the autumn. * One becomes confused among the multitude of roses, I know, but *Nevada* is really so magnificent that you cannot afford to overlook her. A snowstorm in summer, as her name implies. And so little bother. No pruning; no staking; no tying. And nearly as thornless as dear old *Zéphyrine Drouhin*. No scent, I am afraid; she is for the eye, not for the nose.

* For *Rosa Moyesii* and *Nevada* see also pp. 191–3.

November

November 24, 1946

JUDGING by the number of letters I received, my recommendation to plant the Alpine strawberries seems to have aroused some interest among readers of *The Observer*: I now venture, therefore, to recommend the hardy vine, or outdoor grape. I did just refer to this in an earlier article, but as a wall-covering rather than as a fruit, laying very little emphasis upon its edible qualities. It does not appear to be generally known that vineyards were once common in the southern counties, that the grapes ripened, and that wine was made from them; so that what man has done once, man can do again. *

The wine-making part is of dubious value to-day, when wine-making means sugar; but there is no doubt that vines producing small, sweet bunches may profitably be grown against a south wall, say the wall of the house. There are several varieties which may be relied upon to ripen in any normal English summer—the non-summer of 1946 was, in fact, the only summer in which my grapes went mouldy, or shrivelled, or in some other way made themselves entirely useless. Of the several varieties I would recommend, in order of merit, *Royal Muscadine*, *Muscatel*, *Golden Drop*, *Dutch Sweetwater*. *Royal Muscadine* I have found by far the best, though *Muscatel* runs it close.

* Since this article was written a most interesting book has appeared, *The Grape-vine in England*, by Edward Hyams, published by the Bodley Head, 16s., illustrated.

Royal Muscadine, moreover, has a romantic history: it was discovered at Cahors by Henry of Navarre on his way to Paris to become Henry IV of France, and was taken by him from Cahors to Fontainebleau, where it became known as the *Chasselas de Fontainebleau.* It is a Chasselas grape, meaning an ordinary little greenish grape of the type you see so plentifully displayed in greengrocers' shops in France and Italy, but none the worse for that, if you have the patience to pick it off berry by berry, or are so impatient as to cram a whole handful of berries into your mouth at one go. It is well worth growing in our southern counties against a warm wall for it means that you can pile a dish of grapes in August and September on your breakfast table.

The hardy vines are also very useful for making vinegar. You can use any of the hardy fruiting vines for this purpose, but if you want to obtain the real red wine vinegar I would recommend planting *Vitis vinifera Brandt.* This produces a dark, almost black grape, which turns into vinegar by the simple method of squashing the fruit into a wooden tub, leaving it to ferment for ten days or a fortnight, and then straining off the juice into bottles. Do not cork the bottles; put in a twist of paper to keep out the dust and flies.

Figs and peaches will likewise ripen in the south more readily than is sometimes supposed. There is no need to regard them as luxury fruits. The figs *Brown Turkey* and *Brunswick* are especially reliable against a wall.

*   *   *

A small shrub which I should like particularly to recommend is *Caryopteris Clandonensis.* It flowers from August onwards, bright blue and fringed, at a time when flowering shrubs are rare. Prune it, not very hard, at the end of February, and it will make a rounded bush from three to four feet high. If you cannot obtain the variety *Clandonensis,* the sorts named *Mastacanthus* or *tangutica* will do as well. They like a sunny place but are not fussy as to soil; and in order to obtain the best effect I should plant at least three in a clump. At present-day prices, they cost from 4s. 6d. to 5s. 6d.

By the way, are you aware that many of the nurserymen now supply plant-tokens in the same way as booksellers supply book-tokens? The only difference is that whereas book-tokens can be exchanged in almost any book-shop, plant-tokens can be exchanged only at the nursery that issues them; but as the big nurseries have a wide choice of plants and seeds, this restriction does not much matter.

November 24, 1946

From the gardening point of view, those who live in the south of our island have certain undeniable advantages over those that live in the north. The climate is softer; a fact which undoubtedly influences those plants marked by an ominous little asterisk in nurserymen's catalogues, meaning 'Suitable only for mild localities.' Nevertheless, those who live in the north need not despair; indeed, there are times when they may exult, for there are some things they can grow to greater perfection. What about *Tropaeolum speciosum*, the flame nasturtium, with brilliant red trumpets among the small dark leaves? This is the glory of Scottish gardens, defeating most efforts to grow it in the south, even on the cool north side of a hedge. And what about the autumn gentian, *sino-ornata*, which will do also in the south, in a lime-free bed of almost pure leaf-mould, but which is even better in the cooler conditions of the north? There are few lovelier plants for the shortening days of autumn; low, brilliant trumpets of the purest blue, increasing rapidly into large clumps that can be pulled to pieces and replanted or given away.* The coloured primroses

* See also pp. 123–5 and 141–2.

and polyantha also seem to favour a cool climate; indeed, many of the old-fashioned double primroses have now become so rare as to be obtainable only from a few Scottish nurseries.

The tropaeolum, the gentian, and the primrose are plants for every purse; but where a few extra shillings can be afforded they might well be expended on the magnificent Himalayan lily, *Lilium giganteum*, which the well-informed gardener always tried to obtain from Lord Stair's garden at Lochinch, Stranraer. Here, grown in light woodland, they were seen at their best. Eight to ten feet tall, they lifted their spires heavily hung with white trumpets, and as heavily spiced with scent. One of these spires, cut and put in a room, scents the air almost too strongly for the average person to endure.

They are expensive to buy, about 5s. for one three-year-old bulb, that is a bulb of flowering size; but they are more economical than they sound. For one thing, you may buy younger bulbs at a much cheaper rate, and grow them on for yourself; and for another thing, a full-grown bulb (which dies after its first flowering) will give you a whole cluster of little bulbs round it, which you can plant out in a nursery-bed and thus, in three years' time, obtain ten or twelve for a fine group. Dig it up in October or November, to divide and replant. After this, you need never be without them. They like semi-shade; a rich mixture of leaf-mould and loam; manure if you can supply it, buried deep enough for their roots to reach; and a little bracken or other litter thrown over them to protect their tips against spring frost.*

The study of illustrated books, such as Sir Herbert Maxwell's *Scottish Gardens*, will readily convince the pessimistic that a wealth of perennial plants and flowering shrubs will flourish in northern latitudes. This book, out of print, I fear, but obtainable from libraries, is particularly valuable

* See also pp. 205–7.

in that it not only includes many coloured illustrations, but starts off with a chapter on Scottish gardens in general and concludes with a list of shrubs recommended for northern planting. There is also a book by Reginald Farrer, that great collector and gardener, on his own garden in the Lake District. *My Rock Garden* is the title.

November 13, 1949

I have been getting myself into trouble, and must put it right. Writing about quinces, * I said that they were not liable to disease, *so far as I knew*. By that cautious little phrase I hoped to safeguard myself, and indeed my own experience of quince trees and all the books I consulted endorsed my opinion. It now appears that I was wrong. It appears that they are occasionally liable in wet summers to 'a fungus rejoicing in the name of *Entomosporium maculatum*,' which attacks both the foliage and the fruit; also to brown rot, which attacks the fruit; also to a fungus called cluster cups, which attacks the leaves and fruit of both the quince and the medlar. This fungus has an alternative host in the Savin juniper, and spores from the juniper can infect the quince and medlar, or vice versa. The moral obviously, and for once an easy one to observe, is to refrain from planting a Savin juniper in the near neighbourhood. I am much indebted to the East Malling Research Station for all this information.

*   *   *

The medlar is not a fruit I care much about; by the time it is ready to eat, it bears far too close a resemblance to a rotting or 'bletted' pear. It can, however, be made into a preserve, and the little tree certainly has a definite garden value, for in a favourable autumn the leaves turn into a

* See p. 127.

motley of very beautiful variegated colours—pink, yellow,
green, and brown, freckled with the russet fruits which
always remind me of those knobbly objects you see attached
to leather thongs on the flail-like hand-weapons of medieval
warfare.

But although I may have no great affection for the medlar
as a fruit, my affection for the cherry-plum or *Myrobolan*
knows no bounds. I wish it could be planted more widely.
It has every virtue. It grows quickly; it is pretty in the
spring, with its white blossom; it reaches its supreme beauty
when its fruit ripens in mid-summer and its branches droop
with the weight of fruit almost to the ground. The branches
then seem loaded with fat jewels of amber and topaz, like a
tree in an oriental fairy-tale.

It crops generously, most years. Its fruit makes delicious
jam, especially if you put in the kernels of the stones, when
you get a sharp almond flavour, reminding you of kernels
left in apricot jam. It also makes a good hedge. It is, I feel
sure, a tree to plant both for your immediate pleasure and
for the pleasure of your children after you.

Plant the gages, too. The old greengage and all the other
gages, the *Cambridge*, the *Early Rivers*, the *Transparent*.
This (November) is the time to order and plant them.

November 27, 1949

Some weeks ago (to be precise, on page 123) I wrote
that the blue trumpets of *Gentiana sino-ornata* had given
great pleasure during September. I little knew, then, how
I was underestimating their value; so, in fairness to this
lovely thing, I would like to state here and now, on this
eighteenth day of November when I write this article, that
I have to-day picked at least two dozen blooms from my
small patch. They had avoided the gales by cowering close
to the ground, but they had suffered some degrees of frost;
they looked miserable and shut up; I hesitated to pick them,

thinking that they were finished for the year; but now that
I have brought them into a warm room and put them into
a bowl under a lamp they have opened into the sapphire-blue
one expects of the Mediterranean.

This mid-November bowl has so astonished me, and
made me so happy, gazing at it, that I felt I must impart my
delight to other people in the hope that they would begin to
plant this gentian.

*   *   *

It is not easy to find flowers for this time of year. November and December are the worst months. One has to fall
back upon the berried plants, and amongst these I think
Cotoneaster rugosa Henryii is one of the best. It is a graceful
grower, throwing out long, red-berried sprays, with dark
green, pointed, leathery leaves of especial beauty. It is not
fussy as to soil and will flourish either in sun or shade, in
fact, it can even be trained against a north wall, which is
always one of the most difficult sites to find plants for in
any garden. *Berberis Thunbergii*, either the dwarf form or
the variety called *purpurea*, both so well known that perhaps
they need no recommendation, will also thrive in sun or
shade, and at this time of year flame into the sanguine
colours of autumn. They should be planted in clumps in
some neglected corner, and be left to take care of themselves
until the time comes to cut them for what professional
florists call 'indoor decoration,' but what you and I call,
more simply, something to fill the flower vases with. They
have the additional merit of lasting a very long time in water.

The leaves of the rugosa rose, *Blanc de Coubert*, in either
the single or the double form, also turn a very beautiful
yellow at this time of year and are good for picking. This
rose has every virtue; the flowers are intensely sweet-
scented, they persist all through the summer, they are
succeeded by bright red hips in autumn, as round as little

apples, and the whole bush is a blaze of gold in November.
The only disadvantage, for a small garden, might be the
amount of room the bush takes up; it is a strong grower,
like most of the rugosas, and will eventually spread to a
width of four or five feet and to a height of a tall man. It is,
however, very shapely, with its rounded head, and it
never straggles.

November 5, 1950

A correspondent makes the helpful suggestion that I
might write an article on how to fill up the cracks and spaces
in stone paving. I take it that she means either crazy
paving or square stone paving, or paving made from slabs
of cement, poured in on the spot between a framework of
wooden slats and left to 'set' with some wrinkled sacking
laid over them to roughen the surface. This is a very
economical home-made method; it also enables you to vary
the size and shape of the slabs; and, especially if you in-
corporate into the wet cement some small pebbles known
as 'beach' by builders, is almost indistinguishable from real
stone once it has weathered.

I must assume, however, that my correspondent's paving
is already laid, and is just waiting, stark and bare, to be
planted with something that will take away the bareness.
The first essential is that it shall be something which does
not mind being walked upon. There was once a play called
Boots and Doormats, which divided people into two cate-
gories: those who liked to trample and those who enjoy
being trampled. To-day, in modern jargon, I suppose they
would be called tramplers and tramplees; I prefer boots and
doormats as an expression of this fundamental truth. Many
big boots will walk down a paved path, and there are some
meek doormats prepared to put up with such gruff treatment. The creeping thymes really enjoy being walked on,
and will crawl and crawl, spreading gradually into rivulets

and pools of green, like water slowly trickling, increasing in
volume as it goes, until they have filled up all the cracks
and crevices. The thymes are the true standby for anybody
who wants to carpet a paved path.

There are other tramplees also. *Pennyroyal* does not
mind what you do with it, and will give out its minty scent
all the better for being bruised underfoot. *Cotula squalida*
is much nicer than its name; it has tiny fern-like leaves,
cowering very close down; no flower, but very resistant to
hard wear and very easy to grow. All the *Acaenas* are useful;
Acaena Buchananii, a silver-green, or *Acaena microphylla*,
bronze in colour. A pity that such tiny things should have
such formidable names, but they are neither difficult to
obtain nor to establish. John Scott, whose address is given
on p. 235, supplies a useful list in his catalogue.

November 12, 1950

Writing last week in this column about crawly plants to
grow in the cracks of paving stones made me think how
prettily this notion could be extended in a rather original
way. I imagine a level plot of ground, the size and shape
of which would naturally depend upon the space available;
I would hope only that it need not be *too* small. It could
be square, round, oval, or rectangular. It should not be
under the drip of trees, but part of it could be in the shade,
for the shade-loving plants, and part in the sun for the sun-
lovers. I imagine the whole of this plot well dug in preparation, with a couple of inches deep of sharp sand spread on
top of the soil to keep away the weeds, or at any rate to
facilitate their removal. Then you lay your stones, or your
home-made cement slabs as I suggested. Of course, real
stone is the gardener's ideal, but it is expensive, working
out at about ten shillings a square yard, which is more than
most of us can afford.

It will not matter much what you make your paving of,

for it will soon get covered up with plants and will not show through. I imagine that you will keep the middle of this paved plot for walking on, and that you will there plant the plants that do not object to being trodden underfoot and crushed—the thymes, and the small mints, and the other things I recommended. But in this new imaginary garden-plot you will have scope to plant all sorts of things round the edges where they are in no danger of being walked on.

I imagine lumps of Thrift, green cushions of the particularly pleasing sort called *Armeria Corsica*, or the variety called *Vindictive*; I imagine also clumps of the low-growing daisy, *Bellis Dresden China*, as pink and pretty as its name suggests; and sun-roses (*helianthemum*) foaming in all the delicate colours of terra-cotta, buff, yellow, and rose; and the little trailing *Gypsophila fratensis*, a cloud of minute shell-pink blossoms; and some mounds of saxifrage, inter-planted with the tiny iris-like *sisyrinchium angustifolium*, sometimes called Blue-eyed Grass, which sows itself every-where; and I should have also some tufts of the small iris *pumila*, in blue or violet, and a plant or two of the shrubby little *Aethionema Warleyensis*.

The small bulbs would also find a place—the bright blue scillas, the darker grape-hyacinths, chionodoxa or Glory of the Snow, the miniature narcissi, crocuses both spring and autumn flowering. All of them love the cool root-run they find between stones. There is no end to the choice, and no reason why you should not achieve colour and interest throughout the seasons. The main thing to remember is that what you are really trying to do is to make a rock garden on the flat.

November 19, 1950

What, I wonder, do you feel about rock-gardens? Per-sonally, I am against them, even when they are on a very grand scale. They seldom look right. Of course, if your garden happens to include a disused quarry there is nothing you can do but make a rock-garden out of it; but few of us are thus favoured. Most of us are reduced to some lumpy bank, over which we dispose all the oddments of old stone we can collect and plant them up with such common tufts as aubretia and yellow alyssum. It will be an artificial thing, pretending to be something it isn't.

Nevertheless, there is something to be said for rock-gardening provided you do it tactfully and do not pretend to be reproducing a bit of the Alps or the Himalayas or one of the more remote valleys of China where they were never intended to occur. The best claim to be made for rock-gardening is that it enables you to grow things according to the conditions which please them best. You can, in short, make up pockets of soil between the stones to suit individual plants. You can make a pocket of pure leaf-mould for *Gentiana sino-ornata*. You can make a sharp, gritty, sunny pocket for South African bulbs, the *ixias*, for example, or for the Mexican *tigridias*. You can fill one pocket entirely with limy rubble to please your dianthus; and another pocket with peat and leaf-mould to please your shrubby daphnes. In this way you can cut plants off, one from the others. You can prevent them from getting lost, as small things are apt to get lost in the open ground, and can also control any invasive neighbour—a vegetable neighbour, I mean, not a human one or a feline one.

You will observe that not all the plants I have mentioned are Alpines. This is because I never can see why one should be mesmerized into believing that Alpines should be the only occupants of a rock-garden. The only rule to follow, I think, is that whatever looks right *is* right. Obviously, herbaceous plants will look wrong, and so will many of the annuals; but the pockets are ideal places for the small bulbs, nor is there any reason why they should not come up through a carpeting of saxifrage or androsace or arenaria or *Dryas octopetala* or the prostrate rosemary. I like to see the miniature narcissi grown in such a way, and the striped Lady Tulip (*T. Clusiana*), and our native yellow tulip, *Sylvestris*, and the little green-and-white *Tulipa tarda*, sometimes called *dasystemon*, and that lovely Greek, *Tulipa orphanidea*, and the scarlet Persian *Tulipa linifolia*; and some fritillaries, too, not only our native Snakes-head, *Fritillaria meleagris*, but also *F. pyrenaica*, with its odd colouring of bronze and green; and, of course, the little early Iris *reticulata*. But I must desist. The bright picture growing up so rapidly in my mind already threatens to exceed the canvas allowed me.

November 26, 1950

A week ago I was writing in this column about rock-gardens. Wildfire ideas swept across me, like a prairie alight. My own small blaze was not comparable to that. I just got excited about the things one could do in a rock-garden, which is a mild little thing to get excited about; but, after all, the point is not what you get excited about, but the fact that in middle age you can still get excited at all. There is nothing like gardening to keep one young. It is the most rejuvenating of all occupations. One is always looking forward to next year, or five years hence.

I thought I would write this time about dry-wall gardening. Fortunate indeed are those whose lot is cast in one of our counties where low stone walls solidly crammed with soil already form part of the local landscape—in the Cotswolds, for instance. But even if you do not live where you may hope to find a ready-made dry wall, there is no reason why you should not build one in a place which seems to demand it.

A dry wall, it seems scarcely necessary to say, is a wall in which no hard mortar is used to fix the stones, but only soil to set them.

A retaining wall is the ideal, holding up a bank or a terrace, because then you will be able to build it with a *batter*, which in gardening terms does not mean a sort of Yorkshire pudding but a receding slope, lying backwards from bottom to top; this gives strength to the wall, which, if it were upright, would almost certainly fall down in course of time. Tilt each individual stone slightly backwards also, choosing the biggest stones to set along the foot. Fill the space at the back of the wall with good soil, a mixture of fibrous loam (well-rotted turves are excellent), some sharp sand, some peat, and compost if you have it, and also pack every crevice with the same mixture as you go. The more crevices you are able to leave, consistent with safety, the better.

It is a good plan to put in your plants while you build, and far easier and more satisfactory than poking them in afterwards. It enables you to spread out the roots instead of cramming them, and also to water them in, should the weather be dry. Some sort of planting plan in advance is advisable, to get the colours right, and also the shape and habit of the various plants; for example, if you decide to grow some of the *Lewisias*, or the long-sprayed saxifrage known as *Tumbling Waters*, you will not want them to get smothered eventually under a great beard of aubretia.

December

I FIND, and do not doubt that most people will agree with me, that November and December are quite the bleakest months of the year for finding 'something to pick for indoors.' A flowerless room is a soul-less room, to my thinking; but even one solitary little vase of a living flower may redeem it. So in this note I propose to suggest some things that everybody can grow with a prophetic eye on next winter so that the usual blank period may not occur again. These will be things that flourish out of doors. I am not here concerned with greenhouses.

Viburnum fragrans will start producing its apple-blossom flowers in November, and unless interrupted by a particularly severe frost will carry on until March. It is a shrub growing eventually to a height of ten or twelve feet; it is extremely hardy; easy-going as to soil; and has the merit of producing a whole nursery of children in the shape of young self-rooted shoots. Picked and brought into a warm room, it is very sweet scented.

The Christmas roses, *Helleborus niger*, are in flower now. They don't like being moved—in gardening language, they 'resent disturbance'—so even if you will take my advice and plant some clumps in early spring, which is the best time to move them, directly after they have finished flowering, you may have to wait a year or two before they begin to reward you with their greenish-white flowers and their golden centres. They are worth waiting for, believe me.

They like a rather shady place; moist, but well drained. A western aspect suits them. Once planted, leave them alone. They will grow in strength from year to year. I have a plant in my garden which to my certain knowledge has been there for fifty years. It was bequeathed to me by an old countrywoman of the old type, who wanted me to have the enjoyment of it after she had gone.

Hamamelis mollis. This is the Witch-hazel, a small tree which begins to flower on its bare branches in January. It is a real tough, which will grow anywhere—any soil, any aspect—though the better you treat it the better it will do. This applies to most plants, as to most people. The Witch-hazel will give you scented twigs for picking at a very early age.*

Then there is *Prunus autumnalis subhirtella.* This is a little tree which, as its name suggests, ought to flower in autumn. As a matter of fact, in this country it flowers in November or December, and is very useful on that account. Pick it in the bud; bring it indoors; and it will open into a fountain of bridal-looking blossom. It is said to strike very easily from cuttings taken in early summer from the current year's growth. I prefer it grown as a bush, not as a standard.

I should like to put in one last word for that very common plant, the pink-flowering currant, *Ribes sanguineum.* Nothing could be easier to grow, and it is sometimes despised on that account; but those who have the wit to cut some long stems of it in January, and to keep them in water in a dark cupboard, and to bring them out into the light in March, will find not a pink but a snow-white sheaf, a bride's sheaf, to reward them.

December 7, 1947
We are now in process of restoring a small herb garden after years of war neglect. During the war years we man-

* See also pp. 173–4.

aged to keep a table-cloth-sized herb-garden going, just out-side the kitchen door: a few chives, a solitary plant of lovage, some thyme, some apple-mint, and a clump of garlic. This meant that the wise cook could dash out of the kitchen and quickly grab a handful of something that would turn the salad or the sandwiches into something that made guests ask what on earth has been put into them.

My answer to this was always, simply and mono-syllabically, 'Herbs.' Why don't English women use more herbs in their concoctions? They are easy to grow: take up little room, and make all the difference. *Lovage*, with its leaves finely shredded, will convert a dull lettuce into a salad worthy of a good French restaurant. *Chervil* will serve the same good purpose, and has the additional attraction of meaning 'the leaf that rejoices the heart.' It can be made to rejoice the heart also in soups and stews. *Chives*, those little brothers of the onion, are so accommodating that they can be grown even in a window-box in a city. *Tarragon* can be used in omelettes and scrambled eggs with great advan-tage to the omelette and the eggs; and if you put a leaf of it into a bottle of vinegar the vinegar will greatly benefit.

Hamburg parsley is not really a herb, nor is it really parsley. It has a prolonged root like a turnip that has gone in for slimming; can be stored in sand for the winter; and can either be cooked or shredded raw into salads when it has a nutty flavour. The *Cucumber-apple* is not an apple though it looks like a very pale one, but is definitely a cucumber much better than the normal green kind. It, also, can be put into salads. (So can slices of raw apple. Try.)

All these are ideas which lead me naturally on to salads. We all grow lettuces, but why stick always to the same sorts? Why not grow *Green Jade* or *Tom Thumb*, quite as easy as the others and far better. Stout little lettuces, with solid hearts.

December 11, 1949

At this great planting season of the year we should do well to consider the vast tribe of Pinks, or *Dianthus*, for there are few plants more charming, traditional, or accommodating. In old kitchen gardens one used to see long strips of *Mrs. Sinkins* bordering the paths, and what could be more desirable than that ragged old lady heavily scenting the air? She is a very old lady indeed. Some people think she may be as much as 140 years old, though others would make her a mere 80 or so, and say that she had her origin in a workhouse garden at Slough. Whatever the truth about Mrs. Sinkins may be, she appears proudly on the armorial bearings of the borough of Slough, firmly held in the beak of a swan.

She has a daughter, *Miss Sinkins*, less well known, but tidier and more prim in her habits, a retiring Victorian maiden whom you are unlikely to find in a search through most nurserymen's catalogues. In all the pile of catalogues on my table I can find only one nurseryman who lists her;* and he tells me that his stock is small, although he hopes to raise a larger supply next year. Do not worry about this, for there are plenty of the family to choose from. Our native Cheddar Pink, *Dianthus caesius*, is almost as heavily scented as *Mrs. Sinkins* herself, and is as easy to grow.

This applies to nearly all the pinks. They make few demands. Sun-lovers, they like a well-drained and rather gritty soil; and if you can plant them with a generous supply of mortar rubble they will be as happy as the years are long. This means, of course, that they prefer growing in lime or chalk, an alkaline soil; but they don't insist on it; they exact so little that they will put up with almost anything except a waterlogged place. They hate that; and will revenge themselves on you by damping off.

* W. H. Ingwersen, Birch Farm Nurseries, Gravetye, East Grinstead, Sussex.

The only other fault they have, a most endearing fault, revealing an all too generous nature, is that they may flower themselves to death in your service. You must be on the look-out for this, and cut the wealth of flowers hard back to the grey-green clumps, to protect and save them from their own extravagant generosity.

I wish I had more space to write about the pinks. I would like to devote fifteen articles to them. But at least I can recommend a book to you: *The Dianthus*, by Will Ingwersen (Collins, 10s. 6d.). This is the book for everyone who wishes to grow the *Dianthus* in his or her own garden, so Mr. Ingwersen must take my place as an adviser. The illustrations alone are tempting enough, apart from the text, which is informative, practical, and delightfully written.

December 25, 1949

Why was it called golden, and why a bough, that grey-green tuffet, pearled and dotted with tiny moons? Apparently because it will turn golden if you keep it long enough, but as in this country mistletoe usually comes down with the rest of the Christmas decorations it never gets the chance of assuming this different aspect of beauty.

Shakespeare called it baleful; but, as everybody knows, it is possessed of most serviceable properties if only you treat it right. It can avert lightning and thunderbolts, witchcraft and sorcery; it can extinguish fire; it can discover gold buried in the earth; it can cure ulcers and epilepsy; it can stimulate fertility in women and cattle. On the other hand, if you do not treat it right it can do dreadful things to you. It may even kill you as it killed Balder the Beautiful, whose mother neglected to exact an oath from it not to hurt her son 'because it seemed too young to swear.'

The important thing, therefore, seems to be to learn as quickly and thoroughly as possible how to treat it right.

You must never cut it with iron, but always with gold.

You must never let it touch the ground, but must catch it in a white cloth as it falls. This seems easy compared with the first stipulation, since even in these days most people do still possess a white cloth of some sort, a sheet, or a large handkerchief, whereas few of us can command a golden bagging-hook or even a knife with a blade of pure gold. You must never put it into a vase but must always suspend it, and after every traditional kiss the man must pick off one fruit—which is not a berry, although it looks like one—and when all the fruits have gone the magic of the kiss has gone also.

Folk-tales? He would be a bold man who attempted to explain or to explain away such ancient and widespread superstitions, ranging from furthest Asia into Europe and Africa. Mysterious and magical throughout all countries and all centuries, these tales may be read in Sir James Frazer's monumental work in which he honoured that queer parasite, the mistletoe, with the title *The Golden Bough*.

So here let me concentrate rather on some botanical facts which Sir James Frazer disregards, and try to correct some popular misconceptions about the nature of the mistletoe.

We think of it as a parasite, but it is not a true parasite, only a semi-parasite, meaning that it does not entirely depend upon its host for nourishment, but gains some of its life from its own leaves. It belongs to an exceptional family, the *Loranthaceae*, comprising more than five hundred members, only one of which is a British-born subject—*Viscum album*, the Latin name for our English mistletoe.

The mistletoe, as we know it, grows on some trees and not on others. The worst mistake that we make is to believe that it grows most freely on the oak. It seldom does; and that is the reason why the Druids particularly esteemed the oak-borne mistletoe, for this was a rarity and thus had a special value. The mistletoe prefers the soft-barked trees: the apple, the ash, the hawthorn, the birch, the poplar, the willow, the maple, the Scots pine, the sycamore, the lime, and the cedar. It is seldom found on the pear, the alder, or the beech; and is most rare on the oak.

Another popular mistake concerning the propagation of this queer plant. It is commonly believed that birds carry the seeds. This is only half true. What really happens, by one of those extraordinarily complicated arrangements which Nature appears to favour, is that the bird (usually the missel-thrush) pecks off the white fruit for the sake of the seed inside it, and then gets worried by the sticky mess round the seed and wipes his beak, much as we might wipe our muddy shoes on a doormat, and thereby deposits the seed in a crack of the bark, where it may, or may not, germinate.

Such are a few, a very few, legends and facts about the strange and wanton bunch we shall hang somewhere in our house this Christmas.

December 3, 1950

Many people have a limited garden space. They want to make the best of it and to get as much colour and variety as possible, yet the area they command restricts them. They have perhaps a front garden with a path running up it to the front door, and on either side of this path they have either a lawn of grass or some flower-beds, or both; and under the house they may have other beds, with a path running horizontally from left to right. This does not leave much scope for extra plants. I suggest, therefore, that gardening in tubs might be helpful, interesting, and amusing.

You acquire your tubs—barrels sawn in half. I would not paint them in the conventional colour, which in this country seems to be a most virulent arsenic green, swearing violently with all the greens of Nature; I would paint them the colour of coffee with far, far too much milk in it; and I would paint the bands round them the colour of coffee with no milk at all. This neutral coloration makes a much better foil to the colour of flowers than that wicked green.

You must now fill your tubs. Good drainage is essential, meaning a number of holes bored in the bottom, and then a two-inch layer of broken crocks (old flower-pots smashed up), and then a thick layer of fibrous leaf-mould half the tub deep; and then on top of all that the main soil in which your plants will have to grow for years and years. Give them a rich diet. Turfy fibrous loam and some compost and some bone-meal or some hop-manure, and some sharp sand to keep it open, all mixed up together. Fill the tubs to within two or three inches of the top, remembering that the soil will sink as it settles. Then the only thing left to do is to plant; and, of course, to water when watering becomes necessary. This is perhaps the only disadvantage of tub-gardening: you must keep a careful watch to see that your plants do not dry out.

Everyone will have his own ideas about what to grow. Some people will like tulips or other bulbs for the spring, followed in summer by annuals such as the purple petunia, which, sown in May, gives a sumptuous display from July to October. Others will prefer more permanent things such as fuchsias. Whatever you choose, tub-gardening does seem to be a solution for those who have not as much ground space as they would like and who, by setting their tubs where they want them, can prolong the flowering season in many odd corners.

December 10, 1950

A lady writes to ask what she can grow as an edging to her rose-beds. She wants something out of the ordinary, something that will flower all the summer, something that will require no attention, and, of course, it must be a perennial. Is that, she says, asking too much?

This inquiry rather put me on my mettle. I did not dare to suggest anything so obvious as catmint (*Nepeta Mussinii*), which would have fulfilled all her demands with the single proviso that by way of 'attention' she would have to cut it right back to the base in early spring. Clearly, it is difficult to find something that will at least look neat when not in flower. The rock-roses perhaps provide as long a flowering period as anything, but there again you would have to clip them back after their first rush of bloom (which does last for at least two months) in order to make them break out again later on, and this operation might also come under the heading of 'attention.' The Cheddar Pink, *Dianthus caesius*, I thought, would look neat and gay as an edging, with the additional charm of the exceedingly sweet smell from its masses of pale rosy flowers. Two little speedwells, *Veronica repens* and *Veronica rupestris*, would be pretty in their mats of china blue; and the rather taller *Veronica incana*, with darker blue spikes, would offer the advantage of tidy silvery leaves. *Gypsophila fratensis* and *Tunica saxifraga* would both trail in a foam of pink, like small clouds touched by sunset. Or, if my correspondent desired a stronger colour, the low-growing *Viola Huntercombe purple*, most intense and imperial, would glow in a manner to attract notice even from a distance. Or, if she desired no colour at all, the beautifully shaped *Viola septentrionalis*, pure white, with leaves like a violet.

But, I added in my reply to my correspondent, why restrict your rosebeds to a mere edging? Why not allow the plants to encroach all over the beds? It will do the roses no harm, in fact it will supply a living mulch to keep the ground moist and the roses cool at the roots. It was, I think, that great gardener William Robinson who first advocated and practised this revolutionary idea. His roses certainly throve in spite of, or because of, it. When one murmured something about manure, he snorted and said that it was

quite unnecessary. I fancy, however, that in these days of
compost-heaps he would have agreed to some generous
handfuls being inserted as a top-dressing annually between
the plants; or even some organic fertilizer such as bone-meal.

December 17, 1950

Shady places often worry the amateur gardener, but, as
a matter of fact, there are plenty of plants which thrive all
the better for some shade. There are degrees of shadiness,
and I suppose the ideal is a broken light, where the shadow
is not too dense but is still sufficient to give protection from
the hottest rays of the sun. In such a place, especially if the
soil tends to be moist, all the coloured primroses and
polyantha will be happy as a groundwork; and, if really
moist, should be the perfect home for the taller primulas
such as the Japonica hybrids, or the mealy mauve *P. capitata*,
or the yellow Tibetan *P. Florindae*, or the coppery *P.
Bulleyana*. These are all very easily raised from seed or
division. Phlox enjoy shade and a deep, cool soil; so do the
peonies. The columbines will put up with quite a lot of
shade, and there are some very beautiful hybrids: *Longissima*, a fantastically long-spurred golden yellow; *Crimson
and Gold*; *Crimson Star*; and a huge-flowered blue and white
called *Azure Fairy*. Foxgloves are perhaps too obvious to
be worth mentioning, but these also can be obtained now
in different varieties: the Excelsior strain which flowers all
round the stem, and the really lovely one called *Apricot*,
well named, because it is exactly the pinky-amber of a ripe
apricot turning its cheek to the sun. I think also that the
pure white foxglove looks very handsome in a clump,
towering above the colour of lower flowers. All obtainable
from Messrs. Sutton.

If you prefer shrubs for your shady corner or border, the
choice is wide. Azaleas, provided you have a lime-free soil;
rhododendrons, which enjoy the same conditions, are

mostly too space-taking for the average garden. Some of the daphnes are woodland, leaf-mould-loving plants, especially the murrey-coloured *D. mezereon* and its white form, *alba*; and *D. tangutica*; and the fine hybrid, *D. Somerset*. And then there are the hydrangeas, many of which look far better, I think, shrouded in a little dusky mystery than exposed to a glaring light.

I have no room here to go into details about the hydrangeas; I wish I had. The best I can do is to recommend a book just published called *The Hydrangeas*, by Michael Haworth Booth (Constable, 26s.). He has spent many years in expert study, and this is the first specialized work to be written in the English language on the subject. Serious gardeners will feel compelled to add it to their gardening library; and those more frivolous gardeners, who like joky gardening, will delight in his paragraph on page 164, telling them how to produce miniature hydrangeas two inches high in pots.

December 24, 1950

This article will appear, I suppose, on Christmas Eve when nobody's mind is attuned to hard work out of doors. It therefore seems a suitable moment to take up the challenge of a gentleman in Staffordshire who wants me to write something in defence of Lazy Gardeners.

It is an amusing letter, quite indefensible, yet with some grains of truth in it. He toils not, he says, but all the same gets a lot of pleasure from his neglected garden. His trousers become golden with buttercup pollen as he walks across his unmown lawn. He stares out of his windows in astonishment that a fourpenny packet of seed could produce so many marigolds. He has had neither the time nor the energy to prune his rambler roses, but is enchanted to find that they are still flowering riotously. He enjoys the few perennials left by the previous tenant. In fact, he doesn't expect anything to grow and is thrilled when it does.

This not being at all my own idea of gardening, I gasped at first, but on reflection perceived that there was something to be said for his contentions. It was nearly true, as he remarked, that the lazy gardener has time, peace, and leisure to look at his garden, whereas the active gardener has only work and is far too busy to enjoy anything. It was true also, though he did not say this but only implied it, that tidiness could be overdone. Nobody likes to see nettles, docks, or ground-elder; but a certain disorder among the flowers is surely preferable to too rigid a regimentation. Staking, for example, is a thing which requires to be done with a rare tact; one does not want to see the tall asters beaten down in a sodden mass on the ground, but neither does one wish to see them bound to their stake like the head of a birch broom to its handle. As for grass, nothing can excel the beauty of perfect turf; but unless this can be achieved over a wide expanse, I like to see it enamelled with some daisies—not plantains, thank you, or dandelions.

My correspondent has formed the commendable habit of reading gardening books in the winter evenings, even if he has no intention of putting their instructions into practice, which reminds me that I am often asked to recommend a practical, straightforward, comprehensive book and have no hesitation in advising *The Amateur Gardener*, by A. G. L. Hellyer, published by Collingridge Ltd., price 25s. Even if this seems rather expensive I am sure it is worth the money. Eight hundred pages of text and many photographic illustrations.

December 31, 1950

This may seem an odd time of year to write about irises, those velvet-warm flowers we associate with June—the very word *June* warms me as I write it. Outside all is bleak; the grass looks starved and dingy; this wintry weather is as unbecoming to the garden as to the human face. We all looked pinched and shrammed. But the longest night and the shortest day have gone with December 21st; we have left our darkest days behind us.

These reflections have been induced in me by receiving a copy of the *Iris Year-Book*, published by the Iris Society. I suppose we all grow irises, of one sort or another, even if we are neither experts nor specialists. Most of the irises are the most obliging of plants, putting up with poor treatment, asking for little more than a place in the sun, a modest demand, which we should all enjoy if we could get it. All iris growers would be well advised to join the Iris Society, 10s. 6d. for the yearly subscription, which entitles the member to a free copy of the *Iris Year-Book*. Address: N. Leslie Cave, Summerlea, Sugden Road, Thames Ditton, Surrey.

I have written about irises in this column before now, but never, I think, have I mentioned the *Oncocyclus* and *Regelio* species. I hesitate to do so, because they are not so easy to grow, so I write this note only for gardeners who are prepared to take some extra trouble, quite a lot of extra trouble. You should grow them on a raised bed if possible, under a south wall, in very gritty soil with lots of mortar rubble in it because they like lime and good drainage; and mortar rubble supplies both. If you have a warm, sheltered corner under a house wall, where you can build up a little raised bed and fill it with the sort of soil I have suggested, plant a few rhizomes of *Iris Susiana*, the so-called Mourning or Widow Iris, a black-and-white enormous flower, a fantastic flower that doesn't look true, price about 2s. One calls it black-and-white, but it is in fact grey veined with very dark purple, as you can see if it is held up to the light. Seen like this, the veining suggests an anatomical drawing; or, more poetically, the leaden tracing in a stained-glass window.

Plant also a few rhizomes of Charon, or Hoogiana, or Korolkowi. I do not pretend that you will get a lot of bloom, and I do not deny that you may get some disappointments, but the pride of your successes will compensate. The main things to remember are: (*a*) good drainage; (*b*) a sun-baking; (*c*) avoidance of damp in summer, by placing a pane of glass over the dormant rhizome. These irises come from desert countries, so one must try to reproduce their natural conditions as nearly as possible.

A LITTLE FLOWER BOOK

A Little Flower Book

THERE came recently into my possession a little shabby manuscript book. On the fly-leaf was inscribed:

THE
FLOWER GARDEN
or a discovery shewing
What the Power of Man, with the
Co-operation of Nature, can
now (since Man's fall, and
God cursing the earth
therefrom) pro-
duce in propa-
gating and
improving
of Flow-
ers.

Bound in brown leather, it measured only six inches by four, and its 164 pages were filled with a seventeenth-century script, tiny, but of exquisite legibility. Each page had been given its own heading, and moreover had been carefully ruled with red lines to allow for marginal glosses. It was thus a brown and red little book, for the ink also had faded to brown and some of the pages were slightly foxed. I looked at it and wondered.

Quietly, it preserved its anonymity. There was no name, no date, if you except the words Fra^s Wright, Nottingham, 16th March, 1831, written on the inside of the cover. I was not much interested in Mr. Francis Wright, of Nottingham, for it seemed unlikely that without enormous research, possibly into the Nottingham Parish registers, I could ever discover anything about him, let alone find out how the little book had found its way into his library. No, it was the identity of the author I was after. Who was he, this patient, meticulous man, with his beautiful handwriting, his ruler and his red pencil, his extreme neatness, his manifest leisure and his piety? That he was both censorious and pious I quickly discovered from the first page of the introduction, for after a reference to 'this rude lumpe and confused heape' the Earth, which has been brought into form and beauty by Almighty God, he proceeds to a condemnation of his own times, 'wherein Wickedness superabounds and as it were forceth God to withhold the rain, to send the Mildew, the Caterpillar, and other his inferiour officers to correct us.' I turned then to the index, which was characteristically most full and conscientious, and read under the letter H:

Heaven. must needs be hard to obteyn when our Gardens are so difficult to be made and Kept.

The pathos of that entry endeared him to me. Here is a man, I thought, who may be a bit of a moralist, even a bit of a prig, but who does at any rate appreciate the balks of gardening. How well I knew the mildew, the caterpillar and other inferior officers of God! How well I knew how difficult our gardens were to be made and Kept! even without the complication of obtaining Heaven.

Still, I asked myself, fingering his little book, who was this man, and what exactly were his own times when Wickedness superabounded? What sort of a man was he? And when did he live? I imagined some disgruntled old Cromwellian growling round his garden in disapproval of the Restoration and its ways. My quest for his identity followed a detective story on approved lines; I looked for clues. There were references to Sir Kenelm Digby's *History of the Vegetation of Plants*: this, I discovered, had first been delivered as an address at Gresham College in 1661, republished in 1669. Then there was a reference to 'the new-invented cucurbit glasses,' which might be set mingled with honey and beer to entice wasps and flies which waste the store. This, I discovered, was a direct, almost a verbatim, quotation from John Evelyn's *Kalendula Hortensis*, 1664; yet there was no mention of John Evelyn in the text, and no acknowledgment under the letter E to Evelyn in the index. The index was detailed and conscientious. Why, then, did my unknown anonymous gardener suppress this acknowledgment to Evelyn? Had he a mean character, that would not acknowledge a debt to other people? I sought him down his tiny pages. I read his marginal glosses; and in one of these I found one which amused me particularly, because it concerned an ancestor of my own in the way he made his hot-bed: *The Earl of Dorset useth this way*, it said; and that in itself helped me to date my little book by internal evidence.

There were many other references I followed up, until I narrowed the date down to the later decades of the seventeenth century. One linguistic discovery interested me—the word 'avid' written in the same hand on a loose sheet; yet the first mention of this adjective, I found, was given in the *O.E.D.* as 1769. Perhaps my author was an experimentalist in words as well as in horticulture? A man of education evidently; he knew and quoted Greek. He could also command the graphic image: 'You should prune and train wall-trees like the ribs of a skreen fan or ye fingers of a hand displayed.' The Snowflake, which he has flowering in February, he calls 'ye little early summer foole.' He had, I thought, some sense of humour, for he puts ants or pismires, earwigs or battlerwigs, under the heading of 'annoyances.' Anticipating the needs of 1950, he gives directions for growing and curing your own home-grown tobacco. He knew all about cloches, which he calls cap-glasses or casements. He knew about using weed-killer on paths, which, denied our advantage of buying proprietary preparations in a tin, he had to compose for himself: brine, potashes and water, or a decoction of tobacco refuse. He was sceptical about the influence of the moon on seed-sowing, but conceded that gilliflowers should be sown at the full moon to produce double flowers.

He enjoyed experiments. To make gilliflowers large, he says, you use camomile, valerian, flag-roots and celandine leaves, and beat them all into a salve together and apply it to the roots and water them with the same juice, when the gilliflowers will grow to 'a wonderful bignes and sometimes alter the colour thereof'; and similarly if you wish to alter the colour of tulips you must anoint their roots with a mixture of herbs, sheep's dung and pigeon's dung, all beaten up together. A practical man, he has much to say about the sowing of seeds and propagation by offsets, 'only take care that the Dame be not destroyed in her delivery.' A kind-hearted man, evidently, to take so sympathetic a view of women in childbirth. A man of parts, with his Greek and his practical unsentimental love of his plants and his lists of flowers and fruit-trees all growing somewhere in his garden, sometime between 1661 and 1700.

What was he, I still asked myself—this man who kept bees and had his garden, demanding so few tools? A water-pot, a tub, a spade, a pair of shears, some mats to put over tender plants—that was all he required. Who was he, who listed 'the great fox-grape,' the iron-coloured foxglove, the cowslips tawny, murrey, yellow and blush, the great double white daffodil of Constantinople, the apples with their now forgotten names—the Golden Doucet, the Belle Bonne, the Ladies' Longing?

Who was he? I had composed a picture of him in my mind: he wore a big straw hat, and went about his garden grum-

bling against the Government. In his little book he had used
the old word, *grutch*, meaning a complaint; and I thought
of him as a grutching person, perhaps an old retired soldier
or civil servant. Then, to my surprise, I had suddenly to
revise all my ideas. My old Cromwellian vanished in one
revealing phrase, explicit rather than refined. The author
of my little manuscript was not a man, but a woman.

Note to the Little Flower Book

My ignorance and lack of scholarship are much to blame.
One cannot, however, know everything; and I render
grateful thanks to Mr. E. G. R. Taylor for informing me
that I can probably date my little book a bit more closely,
since he says it was Dr. Thomas Burnet who described the
post-diluvian world as a rude lump and a confused heap, in
his *Sacred Theory of Earth*, first published in an English
edition in 1684. This puts my little book to a later date than
1684; it becomes more and more of a chronological detective
story.

What odd things happen when a tiny thing out of the
past comes accidentally into one's hands! What unexpected
connections strike up! Even the mysterious Fra[s] Wright of
Nottingham, that previous owner, has been identified for
me without any research through the Nottingham registers.
I received from his great-grandson a letter accompanied by
a most interesting book on their family history. His great-
grandfather would, he says, have approved of the religious
views held by the author of the *Flower Garden*.

SOME FLOWERS

SOME FLOWERS

Hamamelis Mollis—Witch Hazel

HAMAMELIS MOLLIS is perhaps more familiar to many people when they meet it in a bottle under the name Witch Hazel or Hazeline, but to the gardener it means a small shrubby tree, covered in the early part of the year with curly spider-like flowers on its naked branches. There is a particular charm about all trees which carry their flowers before their leaves, such as the almond or the judas: they have a cleanness of design, undisturbed by tufts of green; they allow us to observe the fine tracery of the twigs, while at the same time offering us some colour to look at. The Witch Hazel is certainly a tree which everyone should grow, for its merits are many, and if it has a fault I have yet to discover it, except that it is a slow starter.

Mollis, a Chinaman, is the best of the family, which includes also two Americans (*Virginiana* and *vernalis*) and a Jap (*Japonica*), and *arborea*, which is the tallest of all but whose flowers are inferior to those of *mollis*. *Mollis* is perfectly hardy and even the flowers do not wilt in a heavy frost. It likes a sunny place, where it has room to develop and although it will not revenge itself upon you by perishing outright in a poor soil but will struggle manfully even against the stickiest clay, it will also show its gratitude for a good loam with some leaf-mould mixed in. Another of its virtues is that it starts flowering at a very tender age, so that there is none of that long weary wait of years until the plant has reached a certain size before embarking on the business which made us desire it. From the very first it is possible to pick it for indoors, and there are few things more welcome at the churlish time of the year when it occurs. New Year's Day may see it open; perhaps even Christmas Day. The queer, wriggly, yellow petals with the wine-stained calyx at their base will last for quite ten days in water, especially if you bring it indoors while still just in the bud, and will smell far more delicious than you would believe possible if you had only caught it out in the cold winter air. So delicious is it, that the owner of one small new tree begins to long for the day when he can cut big generous branches instead of the few twigs which is all that he can get at first. Every one of these twigs, however, will be doing its best, and flowering on all its little length.

The leaves come later, at the ordinary time for leaves, and you can forget comfortably about your Witch Hazel during all the months when so many other things give you flowers for your garden and your vase. You need remember it again only when your supply has failed and in despair you go out to look for something to keep you company indoors. And there they will be, those curly yellow petals, ready once more to scent the room and put brightness on the table.

Iris Reticulata

When flowers come so thick in summer that one hesitates which to pick among so many, one is apt to forget the bare cold days when the earth is a miser offering only one or two, take it or leave it. Wrapped in mufflers and overcoats we go and peer about for a stray sprig of winter-sweet, a splashed and muddy hellebore, a premature violet—anything, anything to fill one solitary glass with some pretence of spring long before spring has really arrived. There are the bulbs, of course, which one has carefully plunged in ashes or placed in a dark cupboard, according to the instructions in the garden books and catalogues: but somehow there is always something a little artificial about any flower which has been compelled to bloom before its time. Even though we may not number ourselves among the rich who languidly fill their rooms on an order to the florist with lilac at Christmas and tulips on New Year's Day, there is still, I think, a great difference between the flowers which we force and those which we have the patience to wait for at their proper season. For one thing, the forced flower always slightly spoils our delight in its outdoor successor when it normally arrives; and for another, the forced flower itself, however welcome, is always something of a fake. To the true lover of flowers, these arguments are disturbingly potent.

The moral of all this is, that we especially welcome any flower which lightens the gloom of winter of its own accord. The more fragile and improbable-looking, the better. Such a flower is *Iris reticulata*. It seems extraordinary that anything so gay, delicate, and brilliant should really prefer the rigours of winter to the amenities of spring. It is true that we can grow *Iris reticulata* in pots under glass if we wish to do so, and that the result will be extremely satisfying and pretty, but the far more pleasing virtue of *Iris reticulata* is that it will come into bloom out of doors as early as February, with no coddling or forcing at all. Purple flecked with gold, it will open its buds even above the snow. The ideal place to grow it is in a pocket of rather rich though well-drained soil amongst stones; a private place which it can have all to itself for the short but grateful days of its consummation.

Reticulata—the netted iris. Not the flower is netted, but the bulb. The bulb wears a little fibrous coat, like a miniature fishing-net. It is a native of the Caucasus, and there is a curious fact about it: the Caucasian native is reddish, whereas our European garden form is a true Imperial purple. Botanists, including Mr. W. R. Dykes, the greatest authority on irises, have been puzzled by the Mendelian characteristics exhibited by this group. Mr. Dykes received bulbs from the Caucasus, which were always reddish, the garden form was purple, and yet the seedlings he raised from the garden form were always reddish again. It was only in the fourth generation, raised from seed, that he re-obtained the purple form, and even that differed slightly in colour from the fixed garden type.

It is unlikely that many of us will wish to experiment with our own saved seeds in this way, but still I throw it out as a suggestion to those who have the inclination and the leisure. (Let me warn those enthusiasts that they will have to wait for at least four years between the sowing of the seed and the flowering of the bulb.) In the meantime I do suggest that every flower-lover should grow a patch of the little *reticulata* somewhere in his garden. The variety *Cantab*, a pale turquoise blue, flowers about a fortnight earlier as a rule; *Hercules*, a subfusc ruby-red, comes at the same time as the type.

Fritillaria Imperialis—The Crown Imperial

Like the other members of its family, the stateliest of them all has the habit of hanging its head, so that you have to turn it up towards you before you can see into it at all. Then and then only will you be able to observe the delicate veining on the pointed petals. It is worth looking into these yellow depths for the sake of the veining alone, especially if you hold it up against the light, when it is revealed in a complete system of veins and capillaries. You will, however, have to pull the petals right back, turning the secretive bell into something like a starry dahlia, before

you can see the six little cups, so neatly filled to the brim,
not overflowing, with rather watery honey at the base of
each petal, against their background of dull purple and
bright green. Luckily it does not seem to resent this treatment at all and allows itself to be closed up again into the
bell-like shape which is natural to it, with the creamy
pollened clapper of its stamens hanging down the middle.

It always reminds me of the stiff, Gothic-looking flowers
one sometimes sees growing along the bottom of a mediaeval
tapestry, together with irises and lilies in a fine disregard
for season. Grown in a long narrow border, especially at the
foot of an old wall of brick or stone, they curiously reproduce
this effect. It is worth noting also how well the orange of
the flower marries with rosy brick, far better than any of
the pink shades which one might more naturally incline to
put against it. It is worth noting also that you had better
handle the bulbs in gloves for they smell stronger than
garlic.

It was once my good fortune to come unexpectedly across
the Crown Imperial in its native home. In a dark, damp
ravine in one of the wildest parts of Persia, a river rushed
among boulders at the bottom, the overhanging trees turned
the greenery almost black, ferns sprouted from every
crevice of the mossy rocks, water dripped everywhere, and
in the midst of this moist luxuriance I suddenly discerned a
group of the noble flower. Its coronet of orange bells glowed
like lanterns in the shadows in the mysterious place. The
track led me downwards towards the river, so that presently the banks were towering above me, and now the
Crown Imperials stood up like torches between the wet
rocks, as they had stood April after April in wasteful solitude
beside that unfrequented path. The merest chance that I
had lost my way had brought me into their retreat; otherwise I should never have surprised them thus. How noble
they looked! How well-deserving of their name! Crown

Imperial—they did indeed suggest an orange diadem fit to set on the brows of the ruler of an empire.

That was a strange experience, and one which I shall never forgot. Since then, I have grown Crown Imperials at home. They are very handsome, very sturdy, very Gothic. But somehow that Persian ravine has spoiled me for the more sophisticated interpretation which I used to associate with them. Somehow I can no longer think of them solely as the flowers one sees growing along the bottom of a mediaeval tapestry. I think of them as the imperial wildings I found by chance in a dark ravine in their native hills.

Note: The disadvantage of this fritillary is that it is apt to come up 'blind,' i.e. with leaves and no flower. I noted with interest that this occurred also in its native habitat.

Fritillaria Meleagris—The Meadow Fritillary

Our native fritillary is one of those strange flowers which does not seem indigenous to our innocent pastures at all. There are some such flowers—the wild arum, for instance, and many of the orchises, whom nobody would take for anything but exotics. The fritillary looks like something exceedingly choice and delicate and expensive, which ought to spring from a pan under glass rather than share the fresh grass with buttercups and cowslips. Its very nick-names have something sinister about them: Snakeshead, the Sullen Lady, and sometimes The Leper's Bell. Yet it is as much of a native as the blue-bell or the ragged robin.

Some people mistake it for a kind of wild tulip, others for a daffodil; Gilbert White of Selborne is one of those who fell into the latter error. Miss Mitford does even worse, in calling it 'the tinted wood anemone.' It belongs, in fact, to the *liliaceae* and so might accurately be called our own private English lily of the fields. Its curious square markings explain several of its various names: *fritillus*, for instance, is the Latin for dice-box, which in its turn had been named from a chess or chequer-board; and *meleagris* derives from the Latin for the guinea-fowl, whose speckled feathers so vividly reminded our ancestors of the fritillary that Gerard in his *Herbal* (1597) frankly calls it the Ginny-Hen flower.

It is unfortunately becoming rarer every year, and is extremely local in its distribution. That is to say, where you find it at all, you find it by the acre, and where you do not find it you simply have to go without. Unlike the orchises, there is no chance of coming across a few here and there: the fritillary knows no half measures. When you have once seen it by the acre, however, it is a sight not likely to be forgotten. Less showy than the buttercup, less spectacular than the foxglove in the wood, it seems to put a damask shadow over the grass, as though dusk were falling under a thunder-cloud that veiled the setting sun. For when it grows at all, it can grow as thick as the blue-bell, sombre and fuscous, singularly unsuitable to the water-meadows and the willows of an Oxfordshire or a Hampshire stream. In wine-making countries one has seen the musty heaps of crushed discarded grape-skins after the juice has been pressed from them. Their colour is then almost exactly that of the meadow fritillary.

In its native state the bulb grows very deep down, so taking a hint from Nature we ought to plant it in our own gardens at a depth of at least six to eight inches. There is another good reason for doing this: pheasants are fond of it, and are liable to scratch it up if planted too shallow. Apart from its troubles with pheasants, it is an extremely obliging bulb and will flourish almost anywhere in good ordinary soil, either in grass or in beds. It looks best in grass, of

course, where it is naturally meant to be, but I do not think
it much matters where you put it, since you are unlikely to
plant the million bulbs which would be necessary in order
to reproduce anything like the natural effect, and are much
more likely to plant just the few dozen which will give
you enough flowers for picking. For the fritillary, unless
you are prepared to grow it on the enormous scale to which
it naturally inclines, is a flower to put in a glass on your
table. It is a flower to peer into. In order to appreciate its
true beauty, you will have to learn to know it intimately.
You must look closely at all its little squares, and also turn
its bell up towards you so that you can look right down into
its depths, and see the queer semi-transparency of the
strangely foreign, wine-coloured chalice. It is a sinister
little flower, sinister in its mournful colours of decay.

Tulipa Clusiana—The Lady Tulip

She is familiarly called the Lady Tulip, but always
reminds me more of a regiment of little red and white
soldiers. Seen growing wild on Mediterranean or Italian
slopes, you can imagine a Liliputian army deployed at its
spring manœuvres. I suppose her alleged femineity is due
to her elegance and neatness, with her little white shirt so
jimply tucked inside her striped jacket, but she is really
more like a slender boy, a slim little officer dressed in a
parti-coloured uniform of the Renaissance.

Clusiana is said to have travelled from the Mediterranean
to England in 1636, which, as the first tulips had reached
our shores about 1580,* is an early date in tulip history.
Unlike Lars Porsena, she has nothing to do with Clusium,
but takes her name from Carolus Clusius (or Charles de

* There is the possible exception of the golden *T. sylvestris*, which
some believe to be a native of England.

Lecluse) who became Professor of botany at Leiden in 1593.
Her native home will suggest the conditions under which
she likes to be grown: a sunny exposure and a light rich
soil. If it is a bit gritty, so much the better. Personally I like
to see her springing up amongst grey stones, with a few
rather stunted shrubs of Mediterranean character to keep
her company: some dwarf lavender, and the grey-green
cistus making a kind of amphitheatre behind her while
some creeping rosemary spreads a green mat at her feet.
The rosemary should normally be in flower at the same time
as the tulip, i.e. towards the second half of April, and a few
neighbouring clumps of the blue Anemone apennina
would associate perfectly both as to colour and to quality
with the small pale bluish-lilac flowers of the rosemary.
A grouping of this kind has the practical advantage that all
its members enjoy the same treatment as to soil and aspect,
and, being regional compatriots, have the air of understanding one another and speaking the same language.
Nothing has forced them into an ill-assorted companion-
ship.

If the extent and disposition of one's garden allows one to
indulge in such luxuries as these little pockets of 'regional
gardening,' how lucky one is! Half the secret of planting lies
in happy association. Some plants 'go' together; others, most
definitely, do not. There can be no rule, for it is essentially
a question of taste and flair, but if a rule can be made at all
it is that Nature's own arrangements are usually the best.
Think only of the innumerable tiny alpine gardens all over
the high pastures of the mountains, to see how perfectly
and effortlessly the job is done. A solitary huge boulder, a
cushion of *silene* pressed against it, a few mauve violas
blowing lightly a foot away, a dab of pink thrift, some blue
lances of *Gentiana verna*, and there it is, complete. No over-
crowding, no anomalies. Just three or four square yards of
minute perfection round which you could put a picture-

frame, detaching them from the sunny immensity and leaving them self-contained, self-sufficient. . . .

In this way one may steal sections out of one's own garden and make self-contained satisfactory small enclosures, such as the scrap of Mediterranean hillside, in which to grow the scrubby lavender, the bushy cistus, the creeping rosemary, the blue anemone, and the slim little Lady Tulip who is more like a boy.

Primula Auricula

Auriculas are of two kinds, one for the rich man and one for the poor. There is no denying that the kind known as the Show auricula, which demands to be grown under glass, is the more varied and exquisite in its colourings and markings and general strangeness. Above the mealy stems and leaves, looking as though they had been dusted with powdered chalk, rise the flat heads, curiously scalloped with a margin of contrary colour, it may be of white or gold or green, or of purple or a reddish bronze, all as velvet as a pansy:

> Their gold, their purples, scarlets, crimson dyes,
> Their dark and lighter-haired diversities,
> With all their pretty shades and ornaments,
> Their parti-coloured coats and pleasing scents. . . .
> In double ruffs, with gold and silver laced,
> On purple crimson, and so neatly placed. *

So greatly did the old florists esteem the Show auricula, that they used to stage it in miniature theatres, something like Punch and Judy, painting pictures in the interior of the theatre in order to give interest to their gardens when the plants were not in flower.

* Rev. Samuel Gilbert, *The Florist's Vade-mecum*, 1683.

But although we may have modestly to content ourselves with the outdoor or Alpine Auricula, we have nothing to complain of, for it is not only the painter's but also the cottager's flower. It is indeed one of those flowers which looks more like the invention of a miniaturist or of a designer of embroidery, than like a thing which will grow easily and contentedly in one's own garden. In practical truth it will flourish gratefully given the few conditions it requires: a deep, cool root-run, a light soil with plenty of leaf-mould (some of the old growers recommended the soil thrown up from mole-hills), a certain amount of shade during the hotter hours of the day, and enough moisture to keep it going. In other words, a west or even a north aspect will suit it well, so long as you do not forget the deep root-run, which has the particular reason that the auricula roots itself deeper and deeper into the earth as it grows older. If you plant it in shallow soil, you will find that the plant hoists itself upwards, away from the ground, eventually raising itself on to a bare, unhappy-looking stem, whereas it really ought to be flattening its leaves against the brown earth, and making rosette after rosette of healthy green. If your auriculas are doing this, you may be sure they are doing well, and you may without hesitation dig them up and divide them as soon as they have ceased flowering, that is to say in May or June, and re-plant the bits you have broken off, to increase your group next year.

It is well worth trying to raise seedlings from your own seed, for you never know what variation you may get. The seed germinates easily in about ten days or a fortnight; sow it in a sandy compost, barely covering the seed; keep the seedlings in a shady place, in pots if you like, or pricked out on a suitable border till they are big enough to move to their permanent home. At one time, auricula seed was worth ten guineas an ounce, so perhaps this reflection ought

to inspire us with some reverence for the quantity which
Nature supplies gratis.

Auriculas have a long history behind them. It is suggested that they may have been known to the Romans, as
a plant whose native home was the Alps. With more certainty we know that they derive their name from the
supposed resemblance of their leaves to the ears of bears:
Oreille d'ours in French, *Orecchia d'orso* in Italian; a somewhat far-fetched resemblance, I think, but one which
obtained general credence. Huguenot refugees popularized
them in England, and by the latter half of the seventeenth
century many new varieties had been raised, to which some
charming and fanciful names were given, such as the Fair
Virgin, the Alderman, the Matron, Prince Silverwings, and
a white novelty called the Virgin's Milk. The most pleasing
and descriptive of all names, however, is the old Dusty
Miller, more pleasing even than the name Vanner's Aprons,
as they were called in Gloucestershire, no doubt in allusion
to the tough leathery texture of the leaves. They appear
also to have been called Baziers, but Baziers is a word I
cannot trace, even in the big *Oxford English Dictionary*.
I wonder if it can possibly have any reference to aprons
made of baize. I don't know and offer the suggestion for what
it is worth. One author suggests, perhaps more plausibly,
that it may be merely a corruption of Bear's Ears.

Punica Granatum—The Pomegranate

Of all fruits the pomegranate is surely one of the most
romantic. I never know whether I prefer it entire, with its
polished leathery rind and oddly flattened sides, or split
open, revealing the gleaming pips, each in its watery en-
velope with the seed visible through the transparency. We
can never hope to grow such fully developed fruits in this

country, but the tree itself is hardier than usually supposed. It will even flower, producing coral-coloured blossoms among the dark pointed leaves; it will produce miniature versions of its fruit in the autumn, too, but it is not for the sake of its fruit that I grow it. I grow it for the sake of its leaves and its blossoms; and for the sake, also, of its reddish twigs in spring, and of the young leaves which are as trans-parent as cornelian against the light before they have pro-perly unfolded. I can think of no other shrub having quite such luminous tips, especially if it is growing above eye-level (as one often sees it on the tops of terrace walls in Italy) so that, looking up as we pass along, we catch it between us and the sun. I give it a warm corner, in the angle formed by a south and an east wall; in the winter I heap ashes over its roots, and provide a warm coat in the shape of a Russian mat tacked across the angle of the two walls. I planted a bush of myrtle beside it, thinking that they went well together both as to appearance and general character, wherein I was indeed right, though it was only some years later that I discovered that some botanists consider the myrtle and the pomegranate to be actually allied. Being no botanist, I had merely remembered the groves of myrtle and pomegranate in which I had slept in Persia.

The pomegranate is a native of Persia and Afghanistan, but has made its way so freely into other countries that it is difficult to say now whether it really grows wild there also or not. Some hold a theory that it has been found in a fossilized state in Pliocene beds in Burgundy, but even without going back to prehistoric times for evidence of its antiquity we can trace a long enough pedigree through history, mythology, literature, and art. It has its name in Sanskrit; it appears in sculpture in Assyria and Egypt; it is mentioned in the Old Testament and in the Odyssey. Nausicaa knew it, and her maidens. In Phrygia it shared with the almond the distinction of having enabled the

virgin mother of Attis to conceive her mighty son by putting
a ripe pomegranate (or almond) into her bosom; in Greece
it was held to have sprung from the blood of Dionysos. The
Romans got it from Carthage, and called it *malum punicum*
in consequence. The sculptors of the Renaissance, like those
of Assyria and Egypt, recognized it as one of the most
decorative of fruits—the symbol of poetry and fertility.
One really does not know whether to call it romantic or
classic: it would provide quite a good starting-point for an
argument on those two eternally disputed terms.

Verbascum—Cotswold Varieties

I suppose every gardener is familiar with the Great
Mullein (*Verbascum thapsus*), that ubiquitous weed which
appears in likely and unlikely places, sometimes in the
middle of a rich flower-bed, where it will profit by the good
soil to grow three or four feet in height, sometimes in a
starved dry wall, where it will not attain more than a few
inches. It seeds itself everywhere, and becomes a nuisance
and a problem, because in good conditions it is almost too
handsome a weed to root out. So handsome is it, in fact,
with its woolly grey leaves and yellow spike of bloom, that
were it not set down as a weed we should regard it as a
decorative border plant. Besides, considered purely as a
herb, it possesses many varied qualifications. There seems
to be practically no ill which its decoctions will not cure.
Mullein tea has a long tradition as a remedy for coughs and
lung troubles; it is also reputed to cure such diverse ailments
as ringworm, warts, toothache, headache, earache, and gout.
There are also other uses to which it may be put. It will
drive away the evil eye. It will dye the hair to a rich
gold, as Roman women discovered long ago. Witches made
wicks from its leaves for their Sabbaths. Poachers threw

its seeds into the water to intoxicate the fish. The poor
wore its leaves inside their shoes for warmth. It seems
ungrateful to consider so serviceable a plant as a mere
weed.

And then again, it goes by so many and such picturesque
names in this our country. Some of these names are simply
descriptive of the plant and its woolly characteristics: Our
Lady's Flannel, or Blanket Herb, or Beggar's Blanket, or
Adam's Flannel. There are other names which derive from
its practical uses: the Candlewick Plant, or Hag's Taper,
with their reference to its utility as tinder when dry.
All these considerations ought to add to our tolerance
of the Great Mullein when it arises unwanted as a grey
and yellow torch in the middle of our carefully planned
garden.

Luckily there are some relations of the common mullein
which we may legitimately grow as border plants, to be
obtained under such names as *Verbascum* Cotswold Gem
or Cotswold Queen. It does not much matter which variety
you specify, for they are all equally desirable. They are all
dusty, fusty, musty in colouring—queer colours, to which
it is impossible to give a definite name: they are neither
pink, nor yellow, nor coral, nor apricot, but a cloudy
mixture between all those. They look as though a colony
of tiny buff butterflies had settled all over them. They
are not to be planted in a brilliant garden of orange
and scarlet, but in some private enclosure where they
may associate with other faded colours which will not
swear at them or put them to shame. Their flowering
season, which is a long one, extends from June into July,
therefore they might well be associated with some of the
old roses, such as Tuscany or the old Red Damask or the
purple Moss.

If only one were as good a gardener in practice as one is
in theory, what a garden one would create!

Do not expect your mulleins to do anything much for you during their first year after planting. They will be too busy making roots and leaves to think of throwing up a flower spike, and if they do throw up a flower spike it will be a meagre one, not worth having, so you had better cut it off and let the plant concentrate all its strength for the next season. Be content, for the first year, with a strong rosette of leaves only, and next year you can look forward to a group of flowers four feet high. You will have to stake them and, moreover, to stake them early, for they are apt to get blown about by any stray wind which may arise. Four or five sticks and some string will do it, and of course if you have time to cut off the seeding stalks the more likely you are to get a second crop. I have very little hope that you will be able to follow my advice. I proffer it only knowing that it is right, which does not mean that I follow it myself. There is always so much to be done, that these small jobs are bound to get neglected. The lupins stand heavy with seed-pods and so do the delphiniums, but where are the necessary two, three, four hours to come from? What chance for the mulleins, who are less showy but more subtle and quite as deserving?

Dianthus Caesius—The Cheddar Pink

> Mid the squander'd colour
>   idling as I lay
> Reading the *Odyssey*
>   in my rock-garden
> I espied the cluster'd
>   tufts of cheddar pinks. . . .

Robert Bridges was not being quite accurate in his statements on that occasion, however tenderly he may have

expressed his sentiments. His Cheddar Pinks did not grow in
a rock-garden at all, but in two long bands down either side
of a path at his home at Boar's Hill. At least, that is how I
saw them. He may have had them in a rock-garden also, but
if so I never saw it. Fortunately for me, the Laureate was not
absorbed in the *Odyssey* that evening, but in an affably
hospitable mood was more disposed to exhibit his pinks to
an appreciative guest. Dressed in the true Tennysonian
tradition in a sort of shepherd's cloak and large black hat,
he had already emerged startlingly from among the
rhododendrons—or were they laurels?—to open the gate
for me on my arrival, and now proposed to extend his
courtesy by taking me round his garden. I was charmed,
alarmed, and rather overwhelmed. He was so old, so tall,
so handsome, so untidy, so noble. And so childishly pleased
with his pinks.

They were, indeed, a revelation to me in my ignorance.
I had seen them growing wild on the cliffs of the Cheddar
Gorge, but had never visualized them massed like this,
giving off their scent so warmly to the summer evening.
The Laureate marched in all his stateliness between them,
pretending to be less pleased than I could see he was. Every
now and then he bent his enormous length to pick some,
snapping the stalks very delicately with his sensitive fingers,
and having collected a generous bunch he offered it to me,
solemnly and even ceremoniously, looking at me very hard
meanwhile as though he were sizing me up, which again
was an alarming experience. 'They make a pleasant tussie-
mussie,' he said as he gave them, and I saw a twinkle in his
eye which seemed to indicate that he was testing me on my
reception of the unusual word. I was far too much intimi-
dated to suggest that a tussie-mussie really meant a mixed
bunch, so I let it go and just said thank you. Looking back,
I think he would have liked me better had I bravely cor-
rected him. He would have been amused. One makes these

mistakes when one is young, as I then was, and over-anxious to be polite.

Next morning after breakfast he took me into his private room, and read me some passages from the manuscript of a poem he was then writing. He expounded his ideas about its peculiar rhythm in terms so technical as to be completely beyond my comprehension. The poem, when completed, he thought would be called *A* (or possibly *The*) *Testament of Beauty*. Again I was alarmed and overwhelmed. It was altogether too much like being growled at by Lord Tennyson in his later years.

Anyhow, he did introduce me to the virtues of the Cheddar Pink, and I immediately ordered a packet of seed and grew it down my own garden path in the same way, not so much from any desire to imitate the Laureate as from a desire to reproduce that same delicious smell on a warm summer evening. And in doing so I learnt from experience a lesson which he had omitted to give me. For two summer seasons my Cheddar Pinks were a great success, and I thought they were going on for ever, but, after that, they died out. I investigated indignantly and discovered that our native pink does die out when planted in ordinary garden soil, i.e. grown down the edge of an herbaceous border as Dr. Bridges was growing it. Its only chance of perennial survival is to live in starvation in a crack of a wall, where it may flourish happily year after year. This does not mean that it cannot be grown down the border path also; it means only that you have to renew your supply by fresh seedlings every alternate year—not an excessive trouble to take, when you remember the grey-green clumps which so agreeably throw up the colours of other flowers, and then the pinks themselves while they are blooming and giving off that special, incomparable smell which for me will always be associated with a June day and the cloaked figure of a beautiful, agèd poet.

Rosa Moyesii

This is a Chinese rose, and looks it. If ever a plant reflected all that we had ever felt about the delicacy, lyricism, and design of a Chinese drawing, *Rosa Moyesii* is that plant. We might well expect to meet her on a Chinese printed paper-lining to a tea-chest of the time of Charles II, when wall-papers first came to England, with a green parrot out of all proportion, perching on her slender branches. There would be no need for the artist to stylise her, for Nature has already stylised her enough. Instead, we meet her more often springing out of our English lawns, or over-hanging our English streams, yet *Rosa Moyesii* remains for ever China. With that strange adaptability of true genius she never looks out of place. She adapts herself as happily to cosy England as to the rocks and highlands of Asia.

'Go, lovely rose.' She goes indeed, and quickly. Three weeks at most sees her through her yearly explosion of beauty. But her beauty is such that she must be grown for the sake of those three weeks in June. During that time her branches will tumble with the large, single, rose-red flower of her being. It is of an indescribable colour. I hold a flower of it here in my hand now, and find myself defeated in description. It is like the colour I imagine Petra to be, if one caught it at just the right moment of sunset. It is like some colours in a rug from Isfahan. It is like the dyed leather sheath of an Arab knife—and this I do know for certain, for I am matching one against the other, the dagger-sheath against the flower. It is like all those dusky rose-red things which abide in the mind as a part of the world of escape and romance.

Then even when the flowers are gone the great graceful branches are sufficiently lovely in themselves. Consider that within three or four years a single bush will grow some

twelve feet high and will cover an area six to eight feet wide;
long waving wands of leaves delicately set and of an exquisite pattern, detaching themselves against the sky or the
hedge or the wall, wherever you happen to have set it.
Never make the mistake of trying to train it tight against
a wall: it likes to grow free, and to throw itself loosely into
the fountains of perfect shape it knows so well how to
achieve. Do not, by the way, make the mistake either of
industriously cutting off the dead heads, in the hope of
inducing a second flowering. You will not get your second
flowering and you will only deprive yourself of the second
crop which it is preparing to give you: the crop of long
bottle-shaped, scarlet hips of the autumn. Preserve them at
all costs, these sealing-wax fruits which will hang brighter
than the berries of the holly. If you have a liking for rose-
hips, you would be well advised to mix some bushes of
Highdownensis with your *Moyesii*, for *Highdownensis*
(which is, in fact, a chance seedling of *Moyesii*) produces
even finer hips—amongst the finest of any roses in cultivation. And if you are going in for mixtures, plant *Rosa
Fargesii* too. This is probably another child of *Moyesii*, of
a lighter and more brilliant shade. I am never quite sure
whether the parent and the child go very well together,
or not. Perhaps not. Perhaps on the whole it would be
better to plant them in separate clumps, with something
dark to divide them, say rosemary, or a couple of Irish yews:
the black-green of the yews would be the ideal background
for the precise and delicate luxuriance which the roses
will throw up.

Both *Fargesii* and *Highdownensis* suggest that *Moyesii*
may produce other children in future. *Moyesii* has not been
for very long in cultivation in European gardens, having
been first observed on the Tibetan frontier in 1890, redis-
covered in 1903, exhibited in 1908 and put on the market
in 1910, so we have as yet had but little time to exploit her

possibilities. It seems to be fairly well established that she will not root readily (if at all) from cuttings, so it is evidently on seed that we shall have to depend, and everybody knows how exciting and unexpected seedlings can be. Every amateur among rose-growers might well make a few experiments.

We already have the variety called *Geranium*, of stockier growth, and the beautiful white *Nevada*, which is not a chance seedling but a deliberate cross.

Even the greatest botanists such as Reginald Farrer derived satisfaction from giving their name to a new plant. It is not given to all of us to find *Gentiana Farreri* for the first time, but there does seem to be some hope for all of us of raising a new seedling of *Rosa Moyesii* from our own garden, however humble that garden may be.

Rosa Centifolia Muscosa—The Moss Rose

There has lately been an enthusiastic revival of what we call 'the old roses,' to distinguish them from the more fashionable varieties, such as hybrid Teas, hybrid Perpetuals, Polyantha, and Wichuriana. I have no wish to disparage these varieties, which include many very eligible things amongst them, but anyone who falls under the charm of the old roses will seldom find his heart among the newer ones again. This charm may be partly sentimental, and certainly there are several things to be said against the old roses: their flowering time is short; they are untidy growers, difficult to stake or to keep in order; they demand hours of snipping if we are to keep them free from dead and dying heads, as we must do if they are to display their full beauty unmarred by a mass of brown, sodden petals. But in spite of these drawbacks a collection of the old roses gives a great and increasing pleasure. As in one's friends, one learns to overlook their faults and love their virtues.

Having enumerated their faults—or, rather their disadvantages—what are those virtues? A sentimental association: they recall everything that we have ever read in
poetry, or seen in paintings, in connection with roses. A
more personal association, possibly: we may have met them,
neglected and ignored in the gardens we knew in childhood. Then, they usually smell better than their modern
successors. People complain that the modern rose has lost in
smell what it has gained in other ways, and although their
accusation is not always justified there is still a good deal of
truth in it. No such charge can be brought against the Musk,
the Cabbage, the Damask, or the Moss. They load the air
with the true rose scent.

The Musk may excel the Moss in this respect, but since
the Moss is only a form of the Cabbage it shares the deep,
velvety scent of its relation, with the added attraction of its
own furry calices and shoots. Nobody knows when first a
Cabbage rose turned itself into a Moss, but the first gardener
to observe the freak must certainly have thought with alarm
that his bushes were affected by some unknown disease.
And so, in a sense, they were. Mr. Edward Bunyard, who has
done so much to restore the old roses to current favour, puts
it neatly in his book, *Old Garden Roses*, 'The moss is a
proliferation of the glands which are always present in the
Cabbage roses.' Proliferation was an unfamiliar word to me,
although the context showed me what Mr. Bunyard meant,
but on looking it up in the dictionary, I arrived at the more
precise meaning: 'Proliferate: reproduce itself, grow by
multiplication of elementary parts; so, proliferation.' Well,
the Moss rose as we know it has proliferated itself from the
Cabbage by a multiplication of the elementary parts or
glands. It seems a dry and rather medical way of putting it,
but how lucky for us that the freak became fixed into a
permanent and enchanting form.

Some rosarians cling firmly to the maxim that the rose

which fades from red to lilac is a bad rose, an undesirable rose, a rose instantly to be abolished from our gardens; but others, less conventionally-minded, hold that the bishop's-purple of its dying hours invests it with a second beauty. In the case of the Moss, we must agree. I have two bushes of the Moss, *William Lobb* (incidentally they have attained a height of twelve feet), and as they reach the stage where some of the flowers are passing while others are still coming out, they look as though some rich ecclesiastical vestment had been flung over them. The dull carnation of the fresh flowers accords so perfectly with the slaty lilac of the old, and the bunches cluster in such profusion, that the whole bush becomes a cloth of colour, sumptuous, as though stained with blood and wine. If they are to be grown in a border, I think they should be given some grey-leaved plant in front of them, such as *Stachys lanata* (more familiarly, Rabbits' Ears), for the soft grey accentuates their own musty hues, but ideally speaking, I should like to see a small paved garden with grey stone walls given up to them entirely, with perhaps a dash of the old rose prettily called *Veilchenblau* (violet-blue) climbing the walls and a few clumps of the crimson clove carnation at their feet.

Rosa Mundi

The Wars of the Roses being fortunately over, making one war the less for us to reckon with, we are left to the simple enjoyment of the flower which traditionally symbolizes that historic contest. The only question is, which rose are we really to regard as the true York-and-Lancaster? For the one which most people hail cheerfully by that name in gardens, very often turns out to be not York-and-Lancaster at all, but *Rosa Mundi*.

There is no adequate reason why this confusion should have arisen, for apart from the fact that they both have variegated petals, the two roses are not really very much alike. The Rose of the World (*Rosa Mundi*) is a Gallica; the Rose of the Wars (York-and-Lancaster) is a Damask, but in case that classification is not of much practical use to you, here are two other ways by which you may tell them. York-and-Lancaster is a very pale pink, almost white; a few petals are variegated, but not all; a washy thing, not worth having. *Rosa Mundi* is far more striking. She is of a deeper pink, and *all* the petals are stained with a true carmine. She is also far more free-flowering. It does not very much matter if people, wrongly, like to go on calling her York-and-Lancaster, as they always do and no doubt always will. What matters is that we can now buy a rose which is variously called *Rosa Mundi* or York-and-Lancaster by the ignorant, and, so long as we are quite sure in our mind that it is *Rosa Mundi* we have acquired, can depend upon getting something which will increase in luxuriance from year to year. Striped and splotched and blotted, this fine old rose explores into florescence in June, giving endless variations of her markings. You never know what form these markings are going to take. Sometimes they come in red orderly stripes, sometimes in splashes, sometimes in mere stains and splotches, but always various, decorative, and interesting. They remind one of red cherry juice generously stirred into a bowl of cream. A bush of *Rosa Mundi* in full flowering is worth looking at. It is not worth cutting for the house unless you have the leisure to renew your flower-vases every day, for in water it will not last. Even out of doors, blooming on its own bush, it does not last for very long. It is a short-lived delight, but during the short period of its blooming it makes up in quantity what it lacks in durability. It gives the best of itself for about a fortnight, and then it seems to have expended its total effort for the whole year.

Perhaps all the foregoing makes it sound rather unsatisfactory and not worth while. On the contrary, it is very much worth while indeed. For one thing, you can stick it in any odd corner, and indeed you will be wise to do so, unless you have a huge garden where you can afford blank gaps during a large part of the year. You can also grow it as a hedge, and let it ramp away. Mix some Moss roses with it, and you will soon have a rose-hedge so thick and romantic that all the nightingales of the neighbouring woods will come to press their breasts in song against the thorns. But the companion which really suits it best is Tuscany, who gets a section to herself in this book.

A word as to pruning. The true York-and-Lancaster scarcely needs any pruning at all, except at the interval of a few years, when the bush threatens to become straggly. *Rosa Mundi*, on the other hand, needs all weak shoots to be cut out after the flowering time is over, and in the spring the remaining shoots should be shortened to within half a dozen buds.

A further word as to suckers, those long, strong, thorny growths which most healthy roses throw up from the base of the bush, and which must be cut away unless the bush is to revert entirely to the original briar (or wild rose) stock on which it has been budded. It is sometimes difficult to decide whether the new shoot is a sucker or a valuable fresh addition supplied by the rose itself. Roughly speaking, a sucker springs from below ground-level (i.e. it springs from the *root* of the rose), and this, although not conclusive, is always an indication that the shoot should be regarded with suspicion. The sucker will usually be found to carry larger and more vicious thorns than the rose proper, and the leaves, if closely examined, will be found to differ. The most useful hint of all was given to me verbally by Mr. Bunyard—one of those simple rules which for some reason are never to be found in books, 'Remember,' he said, 'that a sucker can

never have more than seven leaves on a single stalk, and
that therefore any shoot bearing more than seven leaves
cannot possibly be a sucker.'

Rosa Gallica—Tuscany

I fear that my choice among the old roses may be regarded
as somewhat arbitrary and limited. Limited it admittedly is,
and I regret it. There is scarcely a variety I should not have
liked to discuss, from the tight and tiny De Meaux to the
lyrically named Cuisse de Nymphe Émue, but a sense of
apportionment forbade it. I could not put in too many roses
to the exclusion of other flowers, and this is why I have
restricted myself to *Rosa Mundi*, the Moss Rose, and the
Gallica rose called Tuscany.

There seems to have existed once a rose known as the
Velvet Rose. Nobody knows with any certainty what particular rose was meant by this name, but it is supposed that
it must have been a Gallica. Nobody knows the place of its
origin: was it truly a wilding in Europe, or had it been
imported into cultivation from the East? These are mysteries
which have not as yet been resolved. All that we can say is
that the name is very descriptive of its supposed descendants,
amongst which we must include Tuscany.

The Velvet Rose. What a combination of words! One
almost suffocates in their soft depths, as though one sank
into a bed of rose-petals, all thorns ideally stripped away.
It is improbable that we shall ever lie on a bed of roses,
unless we are very decadent and also very rich, but we can
imagine ourselves doing so when we hold a single rose close
to our eyes and absorb it in an intimate way into our private
heart. This sounds a fanciful way of writing, the sort of way
which makes me shut up most gardening books with a bang,
but in this case I am trying to get as close to my true

meaning as possible. It really does teach one something, to
look long and closely into a rose, especially such a rose as
Tuscany, which opens flat (being only semi-double), thus
revealing the quivering and dusty gold of its central
perfection.

Tuscany is more like the heraldic Tudor rose than any
other. The petals, of the darkest crimson, curl slightly
inwards and the anthers, which are of a rich yellow, shiver
and jingle loosely together if one shakes the flower.

No photograph can give any idea of what this rose is
really like. Photographs make it look merely funereal—too
black, almost a study in widow's crêpe. They make the
flower and the leaf appear both of the same dark colour,
which is unfair to so exquisite a thing. If you saw a photograph you might well wonder why I mentioned Tuscany
as a suggested companion to *Rosa Mundi*. I did so because
these two complement each other so perfectly, both
sharing the same mediaeval quality. Just as the faces
of one century differ in some subtle and indefinable way
from the faces of another century, so do these two
roses differ from any rose which could possibly be called
modern.

As, like *Rosa Mundi*, Tuscany is a Gallica, it needs the
same kind of pruning; it will never make a very tall bush,
and your effort should be to keep it shapely—not a very
easy task, for it tends to grow spindly shoots, which must be
rigorously cut out. Humus and potash benefit the flowers
and the leaves respectively.

Abutilon Megapotamicum or Vexillarium

This curious Brazilian with the formidable name is
usually offered as a half-hardy or greenhouse plant, but
experience shows that it will withstand as many degrees of

frost as it is likely to meet with in the southern counties. It is well worth trying against a south wall, for apart from the unusual character of its flowers it has several points to recommend it. For one thing it occupies but little space, seldom growing more than four feet high, so that even if you should happen to lose it you will not be left with a big blank gap. For another, it has the convenient habit of layering itself of its own accord, so that by merely separating the rooted layers and putting them into the safety of a cold frame, you need never be without a supply of substitutes. For another, it is apt to flower at times when you least expect it, which always provides an amusing surprise.

You should thus grow it where you are constantly likely to pass and can glance at it daily to see what it is doing. It is not one of those showy climbers which you can see from the other side of the garden, but requires to be looked at as closely as though you were short-sighted. You can only do so in the open, for if you cut it to bring into the house it will be dead within the hour, which is unsatisfactory both for it and for you. But sitting on the grass at the foot of the wall where it grows, you can stare up into the queer hanging bells and forget what the people round you are saying. It is not an easy flower to describe—no flower is, but the Abutilon is particularly difficult. In despair I turned up its botanically official description: 'Ls. lanc., 3, toothed. Fls. $1\frac{1}{2}$, sepals red, petals yellow, stamens long and drooping (like a fuchsia).'

Now in the whole of that laconic though comprehensive specification there were only three words which could help me at all: *like a fuchsia*. Of course I had thought of that already; anybody would. The flower of the Abutilon *is* like a fuchsia, both in size and in shape, though not in colour. But it is really a ballet dancer, something out of *Prince Igor*. 'Sepals red, petals yellow' is translated for me into a tight-fitting red bodice with a yellow petticoat springing out below it in flares, a neat little figure, rotating on the point of the stamens as on the point of the toes. One should, in fact, be able to spin it like a top.

Abutilon megapotamicum has a companion, *Abutilon viti-folium*, a Chilean which is more frequently grown, but which is less interesting—at least, according to my taste—with its pale mauve flowers or their white variety.

Primula Pulverulenta—The Bartley Strain

The early years of this century, which introduced such an amazing crop of new treasures to English gardens, produced amongst other discoveries from Western China the Primula known as *pulverulenta*—the powdered or mealy primula. It rapidly and rightly became a favourite, but to my mind at least its crimson head is a crude thing compared with the delicate refinement of the Bartley strain which is its child. Mr. G. H. Dalrymple, who bred the Bartley strain, has been kind enough to furnish me with an account of how it came into being:

'Among the first plants of *P. pulverulenta* raised in this country there appeared a pale pink sport . . . I was so greatly taken with this plant and was so anxious to own it that I tried hard to get seed as plants were then (1912) very expensive . . . I had to use the pollen of the type plant on the pink sport to get seed, and the resulting seedlings gave me ninety-nine per cent type colour and one plant that flowered pink. After some years of work on it I had increased the percentage of pink flowers appearing in each generation until 1921 when the drought killed off every plant except one which produced a few seeds. From these I had about one hundred seedlings to plant out . . . and the following spring I had about fifty per cent pink. Further selecting, and the next generation gave me a better percentage and from these I selected the best and started

another generation which gave me I might say ninety-nine
per cent pink shades. Another selection, and the type plant
completely disappeared and has never appeared since.'

The uninitiated may be surprised at the years of patience
required before any new flower is triumphantly put upon
the market, but Mr. Dalrymple's primula is so lovely, as to
reward him now for any trouble he took to secure it. In its
habit of growth, *P. pulverulenta* resembles *P. Japonica*,
rising in a straight stem from amongst a cluster of leaves,
and then displaying itself in ring upon ring of flowers. No
photograph can suggest what Mr. Dalrymple's Bartley
variety of *P. pulverulenta* is really like. Against the white
floury stem as soft to the look as fur is to the touch, you
must imagine the rings of pink, in perfectly toned association. It is difficult to give any exact idea of the colour in
words; to compare it with the pink of peach-blossom would
be to suggest something far too crude, with the pink of
apple-blossom something far too washy, with the pink of a
sunset-cloud something far too pink; nor is there any rose
which will give me the precise shade I want. It really
suggests a far deeper pink which has been dusted over with
chalk, so that the original colour shows through, behind the
slight veil which has been powdered over it by a puff or a
breath of wind.

There is a way of growing this primula which will greatly
enhance the beautiful straightness of the stems. You should
set it on a steep low bank, so that it appears to rise in tiers
of increasing heights. Thus, the plants towards the top
will tower two to three feet above the ones at the bottom,
creating a sheet of chalky pink, sloping down and far more
effective than an equal mass of uniform height. At the
top of the bank I suggest azaleas of suitable colour; and
there are many.

Only one difficulty presents itself against this plan. It is
the simple difficulty that steep banks usually mean natural

drainage, and that these primulas prefer to grow in places which retain coolness and moisture throughout the summer. Therefore you must be quite sure that your steep bank is as cool and damp at the top as at the bottom, otherwise they will thrive in the lower reaches and die parched at the top. This sounds an impossibly ideal condition to impose, but you can fulfil it if your garden offers a bank facing north, well shaded by trees which protect from the blistering sun. Then both your azaleas and primulas can hide themselves from the midday glare; can flower happily, unparched, unscorched; and can ripen and develop towards another year.

A warning: should you wish to save the seed off your own plants, be careful that the mice do not take it before you do. *Pulverulenta* is the only primula which a mouse will attack in this way.

Primula Littoniana

The amateur gardener does not as a rule trouble his head very much with botanical groupings. Such names as 'scrophulariceæ' and 'crassulaceæ' merely inspire him with boredom and distaste. Yet I suppose that a few of the natural orders are instantly recognizable, and that to the roses and lilies we may safely add the great family of the primulaceæ. Lacking it, we should be without the primrose, the cowslip, the auricula, the polyanthus, and the innumerable varieties of primula.

The absence of the primrose and the polyanthus alone, with their range of colours, would impoverish the spring garden perhaps more than we realize. Consider that we can now grow them in blue, mauve, magenta, yellow, white, ruby, bronze, orange; consider also that they spread their flowering over nearly two months in April and May; that even in autumn and throughout a mild winter you are liable to find a few stray blooms; that they may be increased indefinitely, either by self-sown seedlings or by pulling big clumps to pieces. There are few plants more obliging. The smallest rooted bit will grown, and it is even possible to transplant them while in full flower: they scarcely seem to notice the move. A cool soil and the same amount of shade as pleases our native primrose is all they ask.

Their grander relations, the tall primulas, vary of course in amiability. They are the aristocrats of the group and as such are entitled to their fancies. Some of them, indeed, appear to be so democratically-minded as to accommodate themselves to our wishes as readily as the primrose and the polyanthus; thus, although *P. Japonica* and the yellow *P. Sikkimensis* have travelled across half the world before reaching England, they give themselves no airs on arrival but adapt themselves happily to the banks of our woodland streams, set a lavish store of seed for our use, and quickly grow themselves into dividable clumps as big as cabbages. With these, however, I am not for the moment concerned. I am concerned with the more unusual *Primula Littoniana*,* a native of Yunnan, which many people admire when they see it at flower-shows but seldom grow in their own gardens. It seems to be one of those plants which get so far as the compliment of an X pencilled against it in the nurseryman's leaflet, and stop at that. I do not quite know why. It is a very shapely thing, not difficult to grow with success. My illustration, I think, gives quite a good idea of its quality, though of course not of its colour. The photograph does at least suggest the thimble-like effect of a cone set on the top of the flower, though it necessarily leaves out the red and violet diversity of the half-expanded flower. The photograph suggests also the conditions under which this primula likes to be grown; cool, shady, rather moist, with plenty of leaf-mould for its rather shallow root-run, and protection from

* Now called Viali.

a burning sun. Given these, a colony should flourish, but
do not expect to be able to increase it by seed for it is not
at all obliging in that respect. Your only hope is to increase
by division of a sturdy plant.

Lilium Giganteum *

It is a contrast to turn from such small delicacies as the
embroidery of the old roses, to the towering heroism of the
Himalayan lily. Too splendid to be called vulgar, she is still
very decidedly over life-size. Unconsciously, one sets oneself
some kind of limit as to what size a flower ought to be, and
here is one which exceeds them all. It looks almost as
though she had adapted herself to the proportions of her
tremendous home. For I suppose that there is no scenery in
the world so appallingly majestic as that of the great mountains of Central Asia. Reginald Farrer found her in Tibet,
and any reader of his books will have formed some distant
idea of that remote and lonely region, scarcely travelled and
practically unmapped, where men are few, but flowers are
many, a ravishing population put there as it were to compensate for the rudeness of life, the violence of the climate,
and the desolation of the ranges.

So the Giant Lily, not to be outdone, has matched her
stature against the great fissures and precipices and nameless
peaks. In an English garden she looks startling indeed, but
out there a peculiar fitness must attend her, making of her
the worthy and proportionate ornament, sculptural as she
is with her long, quiet trumpets and dark, quiet leaves.
I do not know to what height she will grow in her native
home, but in England she will reach twelve feet without
much trouble, and I have heard it said that in Scotland she
will reach eighteen.

* Now called *Cardiocrinum giganteum.*

A group of these lilies, seen by twilight or moonlight gleaming under the shadow of a thin wood, is a truly imposing sight. The scent is overpowering, and seems to be the only expression of life vouchsafed by these sentinels which have so strange a quality of stillness. I should like to see them growing among silver birches, whose pale trunks would accord with the curious greenish-white trumpets of the flower-spike. Unluckily, few of us have a birch-wood exactly where we want it; and even though we were willing to make a plantation, the stem of the young birch lacks the quality of the old.

But failing either of these, any coppice say of hazel or chestnut will serve the purpose, which is to provide shade and coolness, for the Giant Lily will stand a good deal of both. Then you must dig out a hole two to three feet deep, and fill it with the richest material you can provide in the form of leaf-mould, peat, and rotted manure. This simple recommendation reminds me of the exclamation of a friend: 'It seems to me,' she said, 'that this lily of yours has all the virtues and only four disadvantages: it is very expensive to buy; the bulb takes three years before it flowers; after flowering once it dies; and you have to bury a dead horse at the bottom of a pit before it will flower at all.'

Up to a point, these remarks are true. A bulb of flowering size does cost five shillings, it does then die, and it does demand a lot of feeding. On the other hand, it will produce a number of bulblets which you can grow on for yourself, thus arranging for an inexhaustible stock. The best plan is to buy as many three-year-old bulbs as you can afford, and also some second year bulbs which are cheaper. By the time your second year bulbs have flowered and died, you will have some third year bulbs ready for your own raising, and then you are safe indefinitely.

Having then dug your hole in October and filled it up

again, you plant the bulbs so shallowly that the tip, or nose, just shows above the surface of the ground. It is wise to throw down some covering of leaves or bracken as a protection against late frosts. It is wise also to put in some tall stakes at the same time as you do the planting, for stakes will be needed, and by ramming them in later on you run the risk of damaging roots or even the bulb itself. When the leaves begin to appear in spring, put down slug-bait for the slugs attack with vigour, and the glossy perfection of the huge leaves is a thing to be jealously guarded. You then wait for June, when you may expect your reward.

In the following October, you dig up the old bulb and throw it away, having first carefully saved the bulblets which you will find clustering round it like chicks round a hen.

Zinnias

Anthologists sometimes take especial delight in quoting the botanical howlers made by reputable authors, but (unless I have overlooked it, which is quite likely), no anthologist has yet put his finger on Walter Pater's howler when in *Marius the Epicurean* he makes his Romans go in search of zinnias wherewith to deck themselves. 'They visited the flower-market, lingering where the *coronarii* pressed on them the newest species, and purchased zinias [*sic*.] now in blossom (like painted flowers, thought Marius), to decorate the folds of their togas.' Now either Pater had some botanical information drawn from Roman historians and subsequently mislaid by us, or else he was merely drawing on his imagination to find a flower which he thought suitable to decorate a toga. If he was just drawing on his imagination, he went absurdly wrong. For as the zinnia is a native of America and Mexico, and as Marius lived in Rome in the second century A.D., Pater is out by

about twelve centuries: he was, in fact, enriching Rome by
a flower from a continent not due for discovery until some
twelve hundred years later. I suppose this must be granted
under the heading poetic licence.

In actual fact, the original zinnia, or *Zinnia elegans*, was
introduced into European countries in 1796, and since then
has been 'improved' into the garden varieties we now know
and grow. Many flowers lose by this so-called improvement;
the zinnia has gained. Some people call it artificial-looking,
and so in a way it is. It looks as though it had been cut out
of bits of cardboard ingeniously glued together into the semblance of a flower. It is prim and stiff and arranged and
precise, almost geometrically precise, so that many people
who prefer the more romantically disorderly flowers reject
it just on account of its stiffness and regularity. 'Besides,'
they say, 'it gives us a lot of trouble to grow. It is only half-
hardy in this country, and thus has to be sown in a seed box
under glass in February or March; pricked out; and then
planted out in May where we want it to flower. We have to
be very careful not to water the seedlings too much, or they
will damp off and die. On the other hand, we must never
let the grown plant suffer from drought. Then, when we
have planted it out, we have to be on the look-out for slugs
which have for zinnias an affection greatly exceeding our
own. Why should we take all this trouble about growing a
flower which we know is going to be cut down by the first
autumn frost?'

Such arguments crash like truncheons, and it takes an
effort to renew our determination by recalling the vivid bed
which gave us weeks of pleasure last year. For there are
few flowers more brilliant without being crude, and since
they are sun-lovers the maximum of light will pour on
the formal heads and array of colours. The disadvantage of
growing them in seed boxes as a half-hardy annual may be
overcome by sowing them where they are to remain,

towards the end of May. Whether we grow them in a
mixture (sold, I regret to say, under the description 'art-
shades') or separate the pink from the orange, the red from
the magenta, is a matter of taste. Personally I like them
higgledy-piggledy, when they look like those pats of paints
squeezed out upon the palette, and I like them all by themselves, not associated with anything else.

As cut flowers they are invaluable: they never flop, and
they last I was going to say for weeks.

Tigridias—The Tiger-Flower

'May be grown with success on a hot, dry border.'

This is typical of the instructions given in gardening
books and nurserymen's catalogues, which make the
Englishman ask himself where he is going to find a hot dry
border in this country. Borders, as he well knows, are more
apt to be chilly owing to the deficiency of sun, and wet
owing to the excess of rain. He thinks with envy of those
strips of soil at the foot of Provençal terraces, which might
well be described as hot and dry, and, as such, fit homes for
such sun-lovers as the Mexican Tiger-Flower. He thinks of
that succession of blazing days, interrupted only by an
occasional thunderstorm. (Thus do we idealize climates other
than our own, and forget the disadvantages against which
we do not have to contend.)

He may, however, take heart, for there are several ways
in which he may improvise or at any rate substitute conditions such as those recommended. It is true that he cannot
provide sunshine when the sun refuses to shine, but he can
at least choose his border where any available sunshine will
strike it, facing either south or east; and he can do a great
deal towards the desirable dryness. He can arrange for
dryness, i.e. good drainage, either by making his border
on the sharp slope of a hill, or by raising it several inches

above the natural level of flat ground on a bed banked up
by a stone (or brick) surround, with a foundation of broken
rubble or ashes under the soil. Both these systems entail
trouble and labour. Far more simply, he can walk round
his house and find a narrow strip of border facing south or
east, which is almost entirely protected from rain by
the overhanging eaves of the house. In such a position,
only such summer rain as is driven in by an accompanying
wind ever reaches the six or eight inches at the foot of
the housewall; and this, provided the soil is sufficiently
light and crumbly, is an ideal position in which to grow
tigridias.

I imagine, therefore, a long narrow bed under the
shelter of the eaves, entirely given up to this brilliant and
ephemeral flower. Let me explain these two adjectives.
Brilliant is frequently used of flowers too rashly and too
unadvisedly, but of the *tigridia* with deserved justice, for a
border of these Mexicans really resembles a colony of bright
and enormous insects, settled upon green leaves but ready
at any moment to be off. They look like gigantic butterflies,
flat, open, wing-spread; white, yellow, orange, carmine,
spotted, speckled, beautifully shaped. But ephemeral, short-
lived. One would expect no less of such a butterfly flower.
Within a few hours of opening, the individual flower has
closed its petals in a saddened droop. Astonishing at breakfast, miserable at luncheon . . . Watching them, it seems
tragic that so exquisite a form of creation should also be
so wasteful, that the surprising bloom which one has discovered in the morning should be gone by the afternoon;
but in splendid compensation another crop of poised insects
is there next morning, like a renewal of reward after brief
discouragement.

The moral of all this is, that the tiger-iris (for *tigridias*
belong to the iris family) should be planted in dozens or in
hundreds. Only by planting a quantity can you ensure a

real display. Each plant will give generously, but it takes a
quantity to keep up the daily, hourly supply. Like dahlias
or gladioli, they had better be taken up for the winter and
kept in a shed where the frost will not injure them and the
mice will not get at them; but unlike dahlias or gladioli,
they give no trouble as to staking, for they grow low to the
ground, a great advantage over those more usual and
obvious flowers, which are to be found in every garden,
where *tigridias* are not.

Gerbera Jamesonii—The Transvaal Daisy

There are some flowers about which there is nothing
interesting to say, except that they happen to have caught
one's fancy. Such a flower, so far as I am concerned, is
Gerbera Jamesonii. It has no historical interest that I know
of; no long record of danger and difficulty attending its
discovery; no background of savage mountains and Asiatic
climates. It carries, in fact, no romantic appeal at all. It has
taken no man's life. It has to stand or fall on its own
merits.

I first observed it in the window of a florist's shop, neatly
rising out of a gilt basket tied with pink ribbons. No more
repellant presentation could be imagined, or anything more
likely to put one against the flower for ever, yet somehow
this poor ill-treated object struck me instantly as a lovely
thing, so lovely that I suffered on its behalf to see it so
misunderstood. I went in to inquire its name, but the
young lady assistant merely gaped at me, as they nearly
always do if one makes any inquiry about their wares un-
connected with their price. 'It's a dysy of sorts,' she said.
It was only later, at a flower-show, that I discovered it to
be *Gerbera Jamesonii*, also called the Transvaal daisy.
Neither name pleased me very much, but the flower itself
pleased me very much indeed. It seemed to include every

colour one could most desire, especially a coral pink and a
rich yellow, and every petal as shiny and polished as a
buttercup. Long, slender stalks and a clean, erect habit.
It was altogether a very clean-looking flower; in fact it
might have been freshly varnished.

The exhibitor was better informed than the florist's
young lady. It was only hardy in this country, he said, if it
could be grown in very dry conditions at the foot of a warm
wall, in which case it might be regarded as a reasonably
hardy perennial. I know, however, that nurserymen are
frequently more optimistic in their recommendations than
they should be, so privately resolved to grow it in an unheated greenhouse. This house is really a long lean-to,
sloped against the brick wall of an old stable, and all along
the foot of the wall runs a bed about six feet wide, which
is an ideal place for growing things such as the *Gerbera*
which cannot without a certain anxiety be left out-of-doors.
I wonder indeed why those who are fortunate enough to
possess such a lean-to, do not more frequently put it to this
use. It is true that it entails sacrificing all the staging down
one side of the house, but the gain is great. Staging means
pots, and pots mean watering, and 'potting on' if you are to
avoid root-starvation, whereas plants set straight into the
ground can root down to Australia if they like. You can,
moreover, make up the soil to suit every separate kind;
you can work under cover in bad weather; you can snap
your fingers at hailstorms, late frosts, young rabbits, and
even, to a certain extent, slugs. There is certainly a great
deal to be said for this method of gardening.

I once saw a lean-to house which had been adapted in this
way, with a special view to growing lilies. The wall had
been distempered a light blue, of that peculiar shade produced by spraying vines with copper sulphate against the
walls of farm-houses in Italy: in the centre was a sunk
rectangular pool, with blue nympheæ growing in it and

clumps of agapanthus at each of the four corners. The tall
lilies rose straight and pure and pale against the curious
blue of the wall. I liked best going into this house after dark,
when the single electric reflector in the roof cast down a
flood-lighting effect more unreal and unearthly than anything I had ever seen.

Salpiglossis

Sooner or later one has to make up one's mind as to
whether half-hardy annuals are worth growing or not.
They certainly take up a lot of time, and once the frost has
cut them down they are gone for ever, and all our labour
with them, for, unlike the hardy annual, they will seldom
renew themselves in their self-sown children the following
year. It is, of course, possible to diminish the labour by
sowing the seeds in the open garden in May, instead of
following the orthodox method of sowing in boxes under
glass in early spring, but then one has to take the risk of a
late frost which may blacken an entire bed of young plants
in one night.

The salpiglossis arrived in this country from Chile as long
ago as 1820 and is one of those flowers which has benefited
incredibly from the attentions of horticulturists to the
original form. There is now nothing which is not entirely
lovely about it except its name. I wish it could acquire a
decent English name, instead of this corrupt Greek (from
salpigx, trumpet, and *glossa*, tongue), but if it possesses an
English name I never heard it. Perhaps when it has been
with us for another century the constant mis-pronunciations
to which it is subjected will produce an unrecognizable
variant, for there are few botanical names which give
greater trouble in the arrangement of their vowels and
consonants. It seems necessary for the English tongue to

put in an additional p or s somewhere. I have heard it called 'salpiglopsis' and 'salsipiglossis' alternately, both, unfortunately, even more hideous than their original. I wonder what it is called in Chile?

Its name apart, it is, as I said, entirely lovely. To my mind it far exceeds its relation the petunia in every way. The range and richness of its colour is amazing. Like the Assyrian, it can come up in cohorts of purple and gold, or in ruby and gold, or in white and gold, when it has the milky purity, gold-embroidered, traditionally associated with the robes of saints and angels. Then you can also grow it in brown and gold, a very rare colour in flowers, for it is a true brown—the brown of corduroy, with all the depth of the velvet pile. The veining is drawn as though by the stroke of a fine brush; and, moreover, suggests what is in fact the truth: that the salpiglossis shows to great advantage as a cut flower. Out in the garden it is apt to look bedraggled rather too easily, for unless it has been carefully staked its brittle stems suffer badly from wind or heavy rain, but in a vase its intense livery glows unsullied. Place it for choice in a window or on a table where the sun will strike it, and then ask yourself whether it has not proved itself worthy of all the care it entailed.

For the same reason, try growing it as pot-plant for the winter months. It adapts itself very graciously to this treatment. Of course you must keep it warm; forty to fifty degrees should be a safe temperature. In fact, you might try rescuing half a dozen plants from the garden in the autumn before the frosts come, potting them, and seeing whether they would not carry on, getting even sturdier as they grew older. Experiments are always interesting, but if you prefer the safer course sow a few seeds in pots in March and grow them on in what gardeners descriptively call a gentle heat.

Lilium Auratum

The various lilies present a problem to the amateur gardener. The advice offered to him by gardening books, nurserymen, and personal friends alternates between divergence and unanimity of opinion, both of which his own experience will prove to be wrong. He is told to plant shallow, and to plant deep; to supply manure and to avoid manure at all costs; to provide shade, and to choose the sunniest site possible. The Madonna lily (*Lilium candidum*) perhaps gives rise to the oddest combination of contradictions. On the divergent side we are told: (*a*) that the Madonna lily revels in a heavy mulch of manure, and (*b*) that manure is the one thing she cannot abide. We are told (*a*) to plant her among other growing things, that her roots may be shaded; (*b*) to plant her where the hot sun will ripen her bulbs. We are told (*c*) to lift the bulbs every two or three years; (*d*) never, at our peril, to move the bulbs at all. On the unanimous side we are told that the Madonna lily is the easiest of all lilies to grow with complete success, a contention which, as every gardener who has not the luck to be a cottager knows, is totally and miserably untrue.

Many explanations have been put forward as to why the Madonna lily reappears triumphantly every year in cottage gardens and peters out in the gardens of those whose home ranks as a house rather than as a cottage. It has been suggested (*a*) that cottagers habitually throw their pails of soap-suds over the lilies, (*b*) that the dust of passing traffic smothers the stems with purifying grit, (*c*) that the bulbs remain undisturbed year after year. Now I should be perfectly willing to throw soap-suds by the gallon over my lilies, and to collect trugs-full of grit for them from the lanes, and, above all, I should be willing and happy to leave them where they were for as many years as they saw fit.

I ask no better. I can imagine nothing which would give me greater pleasure than to see a group of *Lilium candidum* increasing season after season, in the happy confidence that they would never be disturbed so long as I was in control of their fate. I would, in short, do anything to please them, but all my efforts have led me to the sad conclusion that the Madonna lily, like the wind, bloweth where it listeth.

There is a great deal more I could say on the subject of the Madonna lily, but I had started out with the intention of writing about *Lilium auratum*. Less wayward than *candidum*, in fact not wayward at all, there is no reason why the golden-rayed lily of Japan should not grow satisfactorily for all of us. It is said that the Japanese complacently ate the bulbs as a vegetable, much as we eat the potato or the artichoke, until, fortunately for us, they realized the commercial value to European gardens, when the slopes of Fujiyama started yielding a profitable harvest of bulbs timed to reach this country shortly after New Year's Day.

There are two ways in which we can grow this superb lily: in the open, preferably with the protection of shrubs, or in pots. I do not, myself, very much like the association of lilies with shrubs. It always looks to me too much like the-thing-one-has-been-told-is-the-right-thing-to-do. It savours too much of the shrubbery border effect, and suggests all too clearly that the lilies have been added in order to give 'an interest after the flowering shrubs are over.' This is not quite fair an accusation, since shrubs do certainly provide an ideal shelter for lilies, but still I retain a personal distaste for the arrangement. I cannot agree, for instance, that *Lilium auratum* looks more 'handsome' against a background of rhododendron or azalea; I think they look infinitely more handsome standing independently in pots set, let us say, on a flight of garden steps. Of course this method involves a little more trouble. It means carrying the pots to the desired position, and watering them throughout the growing season.

Still it is worth while, and if they can be placed somewhere near a garden bench their scent alone is sufficient justification.

Luckily, they are very amenable to life in pots, provided the pots are large enough and are filled with a rich enough compost of peat and leaf-mould. It is as well to stake them when planting the bulbs, remembering that they may grow to a height of seven feet, especially the variety *platyphyllum* which is the finest of all. White and gold and curly, it unfolds to expose its leopard-like throat in truly superb and towering arrogance.

HIDCOTE MANOR

Hidcote Manor*

HIDCOTE MANOR, through the generosity of that fine gardener, Major Lawrence Johnston, was the first garden to be presented to the recently formed Committee for the preservation of gardens of outstanding merit under the joint auspices of the Royal Horticultural Society and the National Trust. It lies, secluded and remote, in the leafy country on the borders of Worcestershire and Gloucestershire, far from any considerable town, but within a few miles of Broadway and Chipping Campden, along winding and hilly lanes that could be nowhere but in the very depths of England. Its own farm surrounds it, including a tiny hamlet, extremely picturesque with thatched roofs, and cottage gardens in which I suspect Major Johnston of having taken a very practical interest; and from the top of the garden you command wide views over woods and meadows, with not a house in sight, right away to Bredon Hill on the opposite side of the valley. The manor house itself is charmingly unpretentious, in the Cotswold style, with a forecourt, and a chapel on one side.

When Major Johnston first acquired Hidcote forty-two years ago, he had nothing as a basis to his garden except one fine cedar and two groups of beeches. The rest was just fields, and I cannot believe that to any but a most imaginative eye it can have seemed a very promising site. There was no particular shape to it; standing high, it was some-

* Reprinted from *The Journal of the Royal Horticultural Society*, Vol. LXXIV, Part 11, November 1949.

what wind-swept; there was nothing in the nature of old
walls or hedges to afford protection; the soil was on the heavy
side. It must have required immense energy, optimism,
foresight, and courage to start transforming it into what it
is to-day—a matured garden full of variety and beauty, the
achievement of one man in his lifetime.

There are several points of view from which we may consider Hidcote. It appeals alike to the advanced gardener in
search of rare or interesting plants, and on the aesthetic
side to the mere lover of beauty, content to wander down
broad grass walks flanked with colour, turning continually
aside as the glimpse of little separate gardens lures him.
The combination of botanical knowledge and aesthetic taste
is by no means axiomatic, but Major Johnston possesses it
in the highest degree. To my mind, Hidcote is a flawless
example of what a garden of this type should be—but before
going any further it would be as well to define what we
mean by 'a garden of this type,' for Hidcote amongst its
other merits displays a remarkable originality, and thus
should perhaps not be associated with any 'type' at all.

Would it be misleading to call Hidcote a cottage garden
on the most glorified scale? (It covers ten acres, but acreage
has nothing to do with it.) It resembles a cottage garden, or,
rather, a series of cottage gardens, in so far as the plants
grow in a jumble, flowering shrubs mingled with roses,
herbaceous plants with bulbous subjects, climbers scrambling
over hedges, seedlings coming up wherever they have
chosen to sow themselves. Now in a real cottage garden,
where the limitations and very often the pattern—for
example, the curve or the straightness of the path leading
from the entrance gate to the front door—are automatically
imposed upon the gardener, this delightful effect is both
restrained and inevitable: it could not, we feel, be otherwise.
It is very largely accidental. But in a big garden like Hidcote
great skill is required to secure not only the success of the

actual planting, but of the proportions which can best give
the illusion of enclosure; the area must, in fact, be broken
up in such a way that each part shall be separate from the
other, yet all shall be disposed round the main lines of the
garden in such a way as to give homogeneity to the whole.
At Hidcote this has been achieved by the use of hedges, with
openings cut for the convenience of communication, rather
than by the use of walls and gates; tall living barriers which
do much to deepen the impression of luxuriance and
secrecy. In one such enclosure, I recollect, no larger than a
fair-sized room, where moisture dripped and the paths were
mossy and the walls were made of the darkest yew, scarlet
ropes of *Tropaeolum speciosum* trailed all over the hedges,
more amazingly brilliant in that place full of shadows, than
ever it had appeared on a whitewashed cottage in Scotland.

The garden falls into six main portions. First the forecourt, which is lavishly planted all round the walls with
hydrangeas, hypericum (the Hidcote variety), *Solanum
crispum*, magnolias, buddleia, choisya, carpentaria, and
Schizophragma hydrangeoides climbing beyond the first-
floor windows. After passing through the house, you come
out on to the old cedar spreading its branches over a couple
of steps, and look down the wide grass walk which is the
principal axis, terminating in a short flight of steps flanked
by two little summer houses or pavilions with a slightly
Chinese up-tilt at the corners of the roof, and leading finally
to a wrought-iron gate between brick piers, commanding
the view away to Bredon. On the right hand side of this
wide walk, and raised above it, lies a *very* large grass lawn,
oval in shape, with a mound on which stand two or three
big beech trees; another group of beech trees is at the
opposite end; it is spacious, simple, and peaceful. Beyond
this, concealed behind hedges, is the kitchen-garden with
the glass-houses and the collection of old-fashionable roses.
On the left-hand side of the wide walk are most of the little

separate gardens to which I have referred; and beyond
them again, over a little stream gay with primulas, is the
part of the garden known as the Wilderness—several acres
of trees and shrubs, either for flowering in the spring or for
colouring in the autumn.

I am aware that this dry tabulation can convey no idea
whatsoever of the variety and beauty of the garden at
Hidcote. Even now, I have omitted several features, such as
the other wide grass walk between twenty-foot hedges of
mixed beech and hornbeam; and the heath garden; for in
truth, there is so much to say that it is impossible to compress it into a single article. This place is a jungle of beauty;
a jungle controlled by a single mind; never allowed to
deteriorate into a mere jungle, but always kept in bounds
by a master hand. I cannot hope to describe it in words, for
indeed it is an impossible thing to reproduce the shape,
colour, depth, and design of such a garden through the poor
medium of prose.

What I should like to impress upon the reader is the
luxuriance everywhere; a kind of haphazard luxuriance,
which of course comes neither by hap nor hazard at all.

I have already remarked on the originality of Major
Johnston's garden. This originality displays itself in several
ways. We must always remember that the fashion of one
generation becomes the commonplace of the next; but that
is no reason why we should not pay a grateful tribute to the
person who had the first idea. We have all, in these difficult
gardening years, turned towards the flowering shrubs and
flowering trees and the roses-grown-as-shrubs; we have
become used to seeing them no longer relegated to what
used to be called the shrubbery—and a dingy thing that
usually was—but mixed with other plants in that now
almost obsolete thing, the herbaceous border. This method
is now rapidly becoming customary, but I must recall the
comment made on Hidcote by someone who saw it in its

early days: 'This man is planting his garden as no one else has ever planted a garden.' The garden at Hidcote was bare then; it is no longer bare; it is packed and crowded; not an inch of soil is visible; and that is part of its originality.

Major Johnston maintains, moreover, and how rightly, that if you cram your beds and borders with what you do want, there is less room for what you don't want—weeds.

I have heard gardeners criticize the Hidcote garden because flowers of a kind are not grown in bold masses. It is almost a precept, usually a good one, that big clumps are preferable to small clumps, and that if you have twelve plants of a kind it is better to set all twelve together than to divide them into two lots of six or three lots of four. The advantages and disadvantages of this system are obvious: while the plants are in flower you obtain a more showy effect, but when they are out of flower you are left with a blank. Major Johnston has got the best of both methods, by distributing his plants so lavishly everywhere. Thus there is never a vast blank, and never a corner without colour. This must not be taken to mean that no bold massing occurs. It does, in some instances. The 'old' roses are massed, and many hydrangeas; primulas also, along the stream; *Paeonia peregrina* on either side of a path; fuchsias in a special garden of their own; and many other things too numerous to mention. But generally speaking you are likely to find a patch of humble annuals nestling under one of the choicest shrubs, or a tall metallic *Onopordon arabicum* (or was it *O. acanthium?*), towering above a carpet of primroses, all enhancing the cottage-garden effect to which I have already referred.

I remember in particular a narrow path running along a dry wall; I think the gardener called it the rock-garden, but it resembled nothing that I had ever seen described by that name. At the foot of the wall grew a solid mauve ribbon of some dwarf campanula. It may have been *C. garganica* and this, of course, after the Hidcote principle, had been allowed to seed itself also in brilliant patches wherever it did not rightly belong. Out of the dry wall poured, not the expected rock-plants, but a profusion of lavender (the deep Hidcote variety, superior in every way to the common *Spica*) and wands of *Indigofera*; there was *Choisya ternata* also, and some Cistus; and an *Azara microphylla* on the bank at the top of the wall, which had been allowed to grow into a real tree quite fifteen feet in height; and there was a creamy, fluffy apparition of *Hydrangea integerrima* looking over the top of a hedge somewhere; but it is difficult to remember details in a garden so thick with detail. I remember also a particularly brilliant picture composed of Major Johnston's own climbing rose, originally known as 'Hidcote Yellow' but now called 'Lawrence Johnston,' its rich butter-yellow holding its colour splendidly in conjunction with the flame-and-orange of *R*. 'Signora' its next neighbour on the wall. I ought to have taken more notes and trusted less to memory. Above all I regretted the absence of Major Johnston, who had always been my host on previous visits to Hidcote when no thought of writing an article was in my mind. He could have told me much.

No description of Hidcote would be worth anything without mention of the hedges, and here again the originality of the planter is apparent. There is a great deal of yew, but Major Johnston has not been content with plain yew, skilfully as he has employed it. On one place there is a mixed hedge of yew and box, an attractive combination with its two shades of green: he has realized how many different shades of green there are in Nature, not forgetting the value of dark pools of water with their *chatoyant* reflections, and has made use of all these greens in a way that would have delighted Andrew Marvell. Different textures of leaf have also been made to play their part, in the 'flatness' of yew contrasted with the interplanted shine of holly.

Then there is one harlequin of a hedge, with five different things in it; yew, box, holly, beech, and hornbeam. Like a green-and-black tartan.

The hedges of copper beech entirely redeem the copper beech from its suburban associations; they may not inaptly be compared to a Persian carpet with their depths of rose-madder and violet, and the tips of young growth as sanguine as a garnet seen against the light.

There is just enough topiary to carry out the cottage-garden idea; just enough, and not so much as to recall the elaborate chessmen at Hever Castle or the tortured shapes at Levens Hall. The topiary at Hidcote is in the country tradition of smug broody hens, bumpy doves, and coy peacocks twisting a fat neck towards a fatter tail. It resembles all that our cottagers have done ever since the Romans first came to Britain and cut our native yew and box with their sharp shears. This is right for Hidcote, and just as it should be: Major Johnston has used the old tradition with taste and restraint, and has supplemented it with some arches of a serene architectural value.

Nor must I forget the quincunx of pleached hornbeam, set behind the two small garden-houses. It may not be an exact quincunx in the geometrical sense, but the word will serve. It gives a sudden little touch of France to this very English garden. Neat and box-like, standing on flawlessly straight little trunks, it has always been so perfectly clipped and trained that not a leaf is out of place.

I have but barely mentioned the large, thickly planted area known as the Wilderness. This is partly because in the month of June, when I was last at Hidcote, the Wilderness is not at its best; it is either a place for spring, with all its flowering trees, or for August with its massed hydrangeas (not the wig-like *H. hortensis* but the far more elegant *H. aspera maculata*), or for autumn when it becomes a bonfire of colour. I know of its spring beauty only by repute;

in August I have seen the shrubby hydrangeas—and this, surely, is the way to grow them if you have the space, in a bosky place made secret by the overhanging trees, with a trickle of water somewhere invisibly near at hand, and the smell of damp peaty soil. A little later on, before the Wilderness had reached its autumn glory, I remember a huge colony of colchicums as you emerged on to the grass from a woodland path. I noted also a large tree of *Cercidiphyllum*; whether it was *japonicum* or *sinense* I do not know; but there could be no doubt that with its autumn colouring it must present a most astonishing sight. The Wilderness is indeed a worthy imaginative adjunct to the general design of the garden.

But on the whole I suppose it is as a botanist and plant-hunter that Major Johnston would wish to be thought of. He himself has travelled much in search of rare plants, and many others have been sent to him from all over the world by fellow collectors. The hardier subjects resulting from these expeditions are planted out, it may be at the foot of a wall where lights may be propped over them in winter; the tenderer subjects are roofed over in two plant-houses, with open sides throughout the summer. Here, again, I wished that he had been at hand to answer many questions. I remember the big yellow trumpets of a *Datura*, and the hanging bells of several varieties of *Abutilon*; a pale *Plumbago*; great pots of fine specimens of fuchsia, notably a rare variety of *F. corymbiflora alba*; a *Carpentaria* with the widest white flowers I had ever seen; a striped red-and-white gladiolus from Mount Kilimanjaro, it may have been *Watsonioides*; and a general impression of dripping luxuriance, but to speak of these exotic treasures in any detail is beyond my power.

Near the larger of the two plant-houses are the propagating frames and the greenhouse containing the collection of pelargoniums which were on show at Chelsea this year

(1949). We are now in the kitchen-garden, but in this kitchen-garden are many things more worthy of contemplation than cabbages. Major Johnston is no orthodox gardener: he tips out the contents of his cornucopia everywhere. There is, I recollect, a raised circular bed round a Scotch pine, foaming with *Helianthemum* of every shade, a lovely surprise, as light as spindrift, shot with many colours the rainbow does not provide. There is a full-grown pink acacia near by, which I took to be *Robinia pseudoacacia Decaisneana*, judging by the rich pink tassels of its flowers; but I may have been wrong in my judgment, and it may have been *R. hispida macrophylla*. By that time I had become so wildly intoxicated by the spilling abundance of Hidcote that I was no longer in any mood to worry about exact nomenclature, but only in the mood to enjoy the next pleasure to be presented.

There were several next pleasures in that most original of kitchen-gardens. There were nursery beds full of rose cuttings and young syringas. I remembered how, years ago, Major Johnston had sent me off with a huge bundle of syringas, saying, 'Take your chance of these. Some of them won't be worth keeping, but you may hit on some that will do.' He was right. I took my chance, and now have some fine kinds growing in my garden—children of Hidcote which I am proud to possess—a grand double-white, and a true pink one which particularly pleases me.

Down the centre path of the kitchen-garden are the old roses, planted in wide rows three and four bushes deep. Major Johnston grew these enchanting varieties long years before they became the fashion, and his collection includes many which are still hard to obtain. There was the blackish-purple of the *centifolia* Nuits de Young (How did it come by that name? Was it called after Young's *Night Thoughts?*) and the slaty-purple of the *gallica* Cardinal de Richelieu; Roseraie de l'Hay; l'Evêque and William Lobb tangling their long sprays of amethyst; the pink Buttonhole Rose, with its sharp little pointed buds, also called Rose d'Orsay because that famous dandy affected it in his coat. I have never been able to find this in any nurseryman's catalogue. It would take pages to enumerate them all, so let me merely revive the memory of that June day and the loaded air, and the bushes weeping to the ground with the weight of their own bloom, a rumpus of colour, a drunkenness of scents.

It is a welcome thought that this lovely garden is now available to all. There are many lessons to be learnt from it, both for the expert gardener and the amateur. The expert will find his own interests, though I suggest that with Major Johnston's approval a more elaborate system of labelling might be devised, with special regard for the rarer plants. The amateur, after he has considered and absorbed the general beauty of Hidcote—which will take him through hours of a real treat-day—would be well advised to go back and study what he may learn for the benefit of his own garden. We cannot all aspire to gardens like Hidcote, either in extent or in particularity. But, as I have suggested, there is much in the Hidcote garden which is applicable to the more modest dwelling—the cottage, the week-end cottage, the manor house, and such diverse habitations as are to be found in our small country towns and even in the garden city. There are many hints to be taken. Why, I thought, had I not planted the pink acacia instead of the common white one, years ago? and out of this regret came the moral of Hidcote: choose always the *best* variety, or the *best* strain. Do not be content with the second or third best. Grow it under the conditions that suit it best, e.g. I recall a colony of *Primula* 'Garriard' under a north wall, planted in a rich moist bed of peat and sand: those plants were as big as the largest lettuces. I blushed as I looked at them, remembering my own poor starved samples which hitherto I thought were doing quite well thrust into ordinary soil. A made-up bed

of peat and sand and compost should not have been beyond
my scope; it was simply that I had not taken the trouble.

This article must not degenerate into a cautionary tale,
so I desist, expressing only the hope that gardeners and
garden-lovers will visit Hidcote in their thousands now that
it is open to the public.

APPENDIX

Appendix

A SHORT LIST OF NURSERYMEN

FOR SHRUBS, TREES, FLOWERING TREES, CLIMBING PLANTS, ETC.

George Jackman & Sons,
Woking Nurseries,
Woking, Surrey.

John Scott & Co.,
The Royal Nurseries,
Merriott, Somerset.

Hillier & Sons,
Winchester.

Arthur Charlton,
Tunbridge Wells.

R. C. Notcutt,
The Nursery,
Woodbridge, Suffolk.

Donard Nursery Co.,
Newcastle,
Co. Down,
Northern Ireland.

Burkwood & Skipwith,
Park Road,
Kingston, Surrey.

John Waterer Sons & Crisp, Ltd.,
The Floral Mile,
Twyford, Berkshire.

Winkfield Manor Nurseries,
Ascot,
Berkshire.

BULBS, CORMS, TUBERS, RHIZOMES, ETC.

W. A. Constable,
The Lily Gardens,
Southborough,
Tunbridge Wells.
(Lilies a speciality.)

R. Wallace & Co.,
The Old Gardens,
Tunbridge Wells,
Kent.
(Lilies and irises a speciality.)

Barr & Sons,
King Street,
Covent Garden,
London, W.C.2.

Ralph Cusack,
Uplands, Roundwood,
County Wicklow.
(Uncommon things a speciality.)

P. de Jager & Sons,
Regis House,
43–46, King William Street,
London, E.C.4.

Walter Blom & Son, Ltd.,
Coombelands Nurseries,
Leavesden,
Watford, Hertfordshire.

The Orpington Nurseries,
Crofton Lane, Orpington, Kent.
(For irises.)

SEEDS

Thompson & Morgan,
Ipswich, Suffolk.
(A very long list, including many
varieties not obtainable elsewhere.)

Sutton & Sons,
Reading, Berkshire.

Thomas Butcher,
Shirley,
Croydon, Surrey.

Carter's, Ltd.,
Raynes Park, London, S.W.20.

Ryder & Sons,
St. Albans, Hertfordshire.

R. Bolton,
Birdbrook,
Near Halstead, Essex.
(Sweet Pea specialists.)

Dobbie & Co.,
Edinburgh, 7.

ALPINES

W. E. M. Ingwersen,
Birch Farm Nurseries,
Gravetye,
East Grinstead, Sussex.

H. G. & P. M. Lyall,
Mount Pleasant Lane,
Bricket Wood,
Watford, Hertfordshire.

FRUIT-TREES—AND FRUIT IN GENERAL

Rivers,
Sawbridgeworth,
Hertfordshire.

Laxton Bros.,
63H, High Street, Bedford.

GENERAL GARDEN STOCK—*Herbaceous plants.*

It is not possible to give an exhaustive list, as most nurserymen who
specialize in something or other usually carry a general list as well, but
here are a few:

Baker,
Codsall, Wolverhampton.
(Russell lupins a speciality.)

R. H. Bath,
The Floral Farms,
Wisbech, Cambridgeshire.

Robinson's Gardens, Ltd.,
Eltham, Kent.

Blackmore & Langdon,
Bath, Somerset.
(Delphiniums a speciality.)

Wm. Wood & Son,
Taplow, Buckinghamshire.

Kelway & Son,
Langport, Somerset.
(Peonies a speciality.)

ROSES

Archer & Daughter,
Monk's Horton,
Sellindge, Near Ashford, Kent.

Edwin Murrell,
Portland Nurseries,
Shrewsbury.
(Old-fashioned and specie.)

Roses—*continued*

T. Hilling & Co.,
The Nurseries,
Chobham,
Woking, Surrey.
(Old-fashioned and specie roses.)

The Sunningdale Nurseries,
Windlesham, Surrey.
(Old-fashioned and specie roses.)

F. Ley,
Windlesham, Surrey.

Wheatcroft Bros.,
Nottingham.

H. Merryweather & Sons,
Southwell,
Nottinghamshire.

Daisy Hill Nurseries,
(Successors to T. Smith)
Newry,
Northern Ireland.

McGredy & Son,
Royal Nurseries,
Portadown,
Northern Ireland.

Benjamin Cant & Sons,
Old Rose Gardens,
Colchester.

Herbs

The Herb Farm,
Seal,
Sevenoaks, Kent.

Heath and Heather,
Lullingstone,
Eynsford, Kent.

Uncommon Vegetables

Miss Kathleen Hunter,
Wheal Francis,
Callestick, Truro, Cornwall.

Oddments of Useful Addresses

The Royal Horticultural Society—
Vincent Square,
London, S.W.1.
and
Wisley Gardens, Ripley,
Near Woking, Surrey.

Selective Weed-killers, etc.
Plant Protection,
Yalding, Kent.

Hop-Manure.
Wakeley Bros. & Co.,
235, Blackfriars Road,
London, S.E.1.

Cloches.
Chase Protected Cultivation,
Ltd.,
38, Cloche House,
Shepperton,
Middlesex.

Labels.
John Pinches,
3, Crown Buildings,
Crown Street,
Camberwell,
London, S.E.5.
(Acme labels, metal.)